THE COMMONWEALTH AND INTERNATIONAL LIBRARY
Joint Chairmen of the Honorary Editorial
SIR ROBERT ROBINSON, O.M., F.R.S.,
DEAN ATHELSTAN SPILHAUS, MIN
Publisher: ROBERT MAXWELL, M.

HISTORY DIVISION
General Editor: G. M. D. HOWAT

BACKGROUND TO THE
ENGLISH CIVIL WAR

Frontispiece: Charles I and Henrietta Maria

BACKGROUND TO THE ENGLISH CIVIL WAR

by

FRANK W. JESSUP, F.S.A.

PERGAMON PRESS

OXFORD · LONDON · EDINBURGH · NEW YORK
TORONTO · PARIS · BRAUNSCHWEIG

Pergamon Press Ltd., Headington Hill Hall, Oxford
4 & 5 Fitzroy Square, London W.1
Pergamon Press (Scotland) Ltd., 2 & 3 Teviot Place, Edinburgh 1
Pergamon Press Inc., 440–1 21st Street, Long Island City, New York 11101
Pergamon of Canada, Ltd., 6 Adelaide Street East, Toronto, Ontario
Pergamon Press S.A.R.L., 24 rue des Écoles, Paris 5e
Vieweg & Sohn GmbH, Burgplatz 1, Braunschweig

Printed in Great Britain by Dawson & Goodall Ltd., Bath

For

R. A. J.

in the hope that one day
it may all become intelligible

CONTENTS

PREFACE

THE two middle decades of the seventeenth century were as dramatic and as pregnant as any period in England's history: two civil wars; a King executed, not to mention an archbishop; a series of wide-ranging constitutional experiments; violent controversy about religion; the Crown on offer to a commoner; and finally the restoration of the exiled Stuarts. It remains a period of unabated interest, whether at the schoolboy level of cavaliers *versus* round-heads, or at the sophisticated level of the history of ideas. But the kind of questions that interest the man on the Clapham omnibus are, I suppose: What was it like to live through these years of turmoil? What were the issues that men so passionately argued, quarrelled, fought about? What kind of men were they who took to the sword to settle their differences? and What was the mood of the summer of 1642 when fighting began — was it akin to the light-hearted abandon of August 1914, or was it nearer to the sombre unease of September 1939?

This short anthology is an attempt to throw light on these questions by using the words, written or spoken, of the *dramatis personae* themselves. A major problem, at the outset, is to know where to begin. Many of the difficulties that confronted Charles I and his Parliamentarian opponents were implicit in the England of Henry VIII and the Reformation — indeed the seventeenth century crisis can be regarded as the painful transition, in government, from medieval to modern (and not only in government; there is an appropriate symbolism in the rejection by the King of the petition submitted to him by the Midland bowyers and fletchers in September 1642 begging him to fight the war with bows and arrows and so support their declining business).

ix

Some of the selected passages are taken from official documents; others, in which there is a fair element of gossip, from letters and notes of a personal and informal kind. Some, such as the ship-money writ, the Court of High Commission warrant, or the petition by a maimed soldier for a pension, are typical of whole series of similar documents, but others, like the warrant for Charles I's execution or Cromwell's letter to his brother-in-law on his nephew's death, stand alone. Most of them have already appeared in print, although some are not readily accessible, and familiar passages have not been avoided merely because of their familiarity if they seemed best calculated to explain an important fact or attitude.

Another man's anthology is never satisfactory; he puts in some of the wrong things, and omits some of those that are essential. In an anthology of literary work disagreement about what should be included and what should be left out is mainly a matter of taste. In this kind of anthology the selection may reflect the compiler's taste, but more significantly it reveals his own views as to what is important, what is enlightening, what is interesting. Even if the selection could be performed on some sort of mechanical, dehumanised, scientifically balanced basis, such a book could not tell the truth, the whole truth, and nothing but the truth about the Civil War, for we cannot take any of these statements at its face value. Of every passage we must ask: what opportunity did the writer have of knowing these alleged facts, how long after the event was he speaking or writing, to whom, and — often a revealing question — why was he making the statement? We may then sometimes conclude that the passage is unsatisfactory evidence for the facts it alleges but highly informative about what the author believed and thought; and that, as Collingwood said at one time, *is* history — "getting inside other people's heads, looking at their situation through their eyes, and thinking for yourself whether the way they tackled it was the right way".

Except in two instances when it would have been exceptionally heavy-handed to do so, I have tried to bring spelling and punctuation more or less into line with current orthodox practice, without aiming at rigid consistency. Editorial additions are enclosed within

square brackets. The order is broadly chronological, but passages
dealing with the same topic have been brought together even at
the expense of infringing strict chronological order. Brief head-
notes have been inserted to set extracts in their context, but the
book makes no pretence to be a coherent and comprehensive history
of the mid-seventeenth-century generation; if it were, certain
matters, such as religion, the King's prerogative and the Law,
Scotland and Ireland, which are no more than touched on here,
would require much fuller treatment. Its relation to history is
much the same as that of a modern newspaper — it seeks to inform,
though partially and incompletely, and sometimes to entertain.

I could not have put this book together without the help of my
wife, to whom I make the usual acknowledment with unusual
sincerity. The book was initially planned to accompany the
Rediffusion Television series *Royalist and Roundhead*, and I take
this opportunity of expressing thanks to my friends in the company,
and especially to Mr. Guthrie Moir, Mr. Peter Hunt, and Mr.
Edward Hayward, for assistance in various ways.

F. W. J.

Thame, Oxon.,
January 1966.

ACKNOWLEDGMENTS

THE author and the publisher thank the *Radio Times* Hulton Picture Library, Rediffusion Television Ltd., Paul Popper Ltd., Mustograph Ltd., and St. John's College, Oxford for their help in providing illustrations. John Glover's *The House of Commons in Session* is reproduced by courtesy of the Trustees of the British Museum. Cromwell's victory commemoration medal and the portraits of Edward Hyde, Earl of Clarendon, and Charles II are reproduced by courtesy of the National Portrait Gallery.

THE STUARTS ARRIVE
AND DIFFERENCES APPEAR

POEM ON THE ACCESSION OF KING JAMES I

Hail, mortal god! England's true joy! great King
All hail! Thy coming forceth my Muse to sing.

.   .   .   .

All wish him welcome, 'mongst all sorts of men,
Save only such as are past sixty-ten:
These wayward old ones grudge to leave behind
What our succeeding Age is sure to find:
The peace, the plenty, pleasure, and such like gain
Which we are sure t'enjoy in James his reign.

JOHN SAVILE (1603)

THE KING AND THE LAW

The twelve judges of the realm are as the twelve lions under
Solomon's throne. They must be lions, but yet lions under the
throne, being circumspect that they do not check or oppose any
points of sovereignty.

SIR FRANCIS BACON, Solicitor-General (1607)

The King is under God and the Law.

SIR EDWARD COKE, Chief Justice of the Common
Pleas (1607)

1

JAMES I IN THE STAR CHAMBER, 20th JUNE 1616

Kings properly are judges, and judgment properly belongs to them from God: for Kings sit in the throne of God, and thence all judgment is derived. It is atheism and blasphemy to dispute what God can do; so it is presumption and high contempt in a subject to dispute what a King can do, or say that a King cannot do this or that.

RELIGIOUS CHARACTERS

A Puritan is such another thing
As says, with all his heart, "God save the King
And all his issue!" and to make this good
Will freely spend his money and his blood.

. . . .

A Protestant is such another thing
As makes, within his heart, God of the King;
And (as if he did, with his Crown, inherit
A never-erring and infallible spirit)
Labours to blow him up by praise of wit,
And by false flatteries cosen him of it.

. . . .

A Romanist is such another thing
As would, with all his heart, murder the King.

The Interpreter (1622)

THE CHARACTER OF JAMES I

He was of a middle stature, more corpulent through his clothes than in his body, yet fat enough, his clothes ever being made large and easy, the doublets quilted for stiletto proof, his breeches in great pleats and full stuffed. He was naturally of a timorous disposition, which was the reason of his quilted doublets . . . His tongue too large for his mouth, which ever made him speak full in the mouth, and made him drink very uncomely, as if eating his drink, which came out into the cup of each side of his mouth. His skin was as soft as Taffeta Sarsnet, which felt so because he never washed his hands, only rubbed his fingers ends slightly with the wet end of a napkin . . . He was very temperate in his exercises and in his diet, and not intemperate in his drinking; however, in his old age, and Buckingham's jovial suppers, when he had any turn to do with him, made him sometimes overtaken, which he would the very next day remember and repent with tears . . . He was very constant in all things, his favourites excepted, in which he loved change . . . In his diet, apparel and journeys he was very constant: in his apparel so constant as, by his good will, he would never change his clothes until worn out to very rags . . . His diet and journeys were so constant that the best observing courtier of our time was wont to say, were he asleep seven years and then awakened, he would tell where the King every day had been, and every dish he had had at his table.

He was not very uxorious . . . he was ever best when furthest from the Queen . . . He naturally loved not the sight of a soldier, nor of any valiant man . . .

He was very witty, and had as many ready witty jests as any man living, at which he would not smile himself, but deliver them in a grave and serious manner. He was very liberal, of what he had not in his own gripe, and would rather part with 100 li. he never had in his keeping than one twenty-shillings piece within his own custody. He spent much and had much use of his subjects' purses, which bred some clashings with them in Parliament, yet would always come off, and end with a sweet and plausible close . . .

He was so crafty and cunning in petty things, as the circumventing any great man, the change of a favourite, etc., insomuch a very wise man was wont to say, he believed him the wisest fool in Christendom, meaning him wise in small things, but a fool in weighty affairs . . .

In a word, he was (take him altogether and not in pieces) such a King, I wish this Kingdom have never any worse, on the condition, not any better; for he lived in peace, died in peace, and left all his Kingdoms in a peaceable condition, with his own motto: *Beati Pacifici*.

SIR ANTHONY WELDON, *The Court and Character of King James* (pubd. 1650)

CHARLES I, HIS WIFE, AND
HIS MOTHER-IN-LAW

THE CHARACTER OF CHARLES I

... He was very punctual and regular in his devotions, so that he was never known to enter upon his recreations or sports, though never so early in the morning, before he had been at public prayers ... he could never endure any light or profane word in religion, with what sharpness of wit soever it was covered: and though he was well pleased and delighted with reading verses made upon any occasion, no man durst bring before him anything that was profane or unclean, that kind of wit never had any countenance then. He was so great an example of conjugal affection that they who did not imitate him in that particular did not brag of their liberty, and he did not only permit, but direct, his Bishops to prosecute those scandalous vices in the Ecclesiastical Courts, against persons of eminence and near relation to his service.

His kingly virtues had some mixture and alloy that hindered them from shining in full lustre and from producing those fruits they should have been attended with; he was not in his nature bountiful ... he paused too long in giving, which made those to whom he gave less sensible of the benefit. He kept state to the full, which made his Court very orderly, no man presuming to be in a place where he had no pretence to be; he saw and observed men long before he received any about his person, and did not love strangers nor very confident men. He was a patient hearer of causes, which he frequently accustomed himself to at the Council Board, and judged very well, and was dexterous in the mediating part, so that he often put an end to causes by persuasion ... He was very fearless in his person, but not enterprising, and had an excellent understanding, but was not confident enough of it: which made him often times change his own opinion for a worse, and follow the advice of a man that did not judge so well as himself: and this made him more irresolute than the conjuncture of his affairs would admit. If he had been of a rougher and more imperious nature he would have found more respect and duty . . .

. . . it is most certain that in that very hour when he was wickedly murdered in the sight of the sun, he had as great a share in the hearts and affections of his subjects in general, was as much beloved, esteemed and longed for by the people in general of the three nations as any of his predecessors had ever been. To conclude, he was the worthiest gentleman, the best master, the best friend, the best husband, the best father and the best Christian, that the Age in which he lived had produced, and if he was not the best King, if he was without some parts and qualities which have made some Kings great and happy, no other Prince was ever unhappy who was possessed of half his virtues and endowments, and so much without any kind of vice.

CLARENDON, *History of the Rebellion* (1646–71; pubd. 1702–4)

His appetite was to plain meats, and though he took a good quantity thereof, yet it was suitable to an easy digestion. He seldom ate of above three dishes at most, nor drank above thrice; a glass of small beer, another of claret wine, and the last of water; he ate suppers as well as dinners heartily, but betwixt meals he never meddled with anything. Fruit he would eat plentifully, and with this regularity he moved as steadily as a star follows its course. His deportment was very majestic . . . for though he was far from pride, yet he was careful of majesty, and would be approached with respect and reverence . . .With any artist, or good mechanic, traveller, or scholar, he would discourse freely; and as he was commonly improved by them, so he often gave light to them in their own art or knowledge . . . His way of arguing was very civil and patient, for he seldom contradicted another by his authority, but by his reason: nor did he by any petulant dislike quash another's arguments; and he offered his exception by this civil introduction, *By your favour, Sir, I think otherwise, on this or that ground:* yet he would discountenance any bold or forward address unto him.

SIR PHILIP WARWICK (1609-83), *Memoirs* (pubd. 1701)

THE QUEEN

. . . the King had another instigator of his own violent purpose, more powerful than all the rest, and that was the Queen . . . the Kingdom is never in any happy place when the hands which were made only for distaffs affect the management of sceptres . . . and it hath been observed that a French queen never brought any happiness to England. Some kind of fatality, too, the English imagined to be in the name of Marie, which it is said the King rather chose to have her called by than the other, Henrietta, because the land should find a blessing in that name, which had been more unfortunate; but it was not in his power, though a great prince, to control destiny.

LUCY HUTCHINSON, *Memoirs of Colonel Hutchinson* (*c.* 1665; pubd. 1806)

THE QUEEN'S MOTHER'S WAYS
NOT INGRATIATING

Henry Oxinden to Thomas Barrow (? August 1641)

. . . The Queen Mother [*i.e.* the mother of Henrietta Maria, and Charles's mother-in-law] arrived at Dover about 7 of the clock upon Saturday night; she made some stay against Sir Thomas Wilford's Welke woods, where she had some fruit which came from my brother Bargrave's presented unto her; I saw her take a pear, and her two dogs drink some water, but somewhat disdainful in regard the glass where the water was in was not brought upon a silver plate, which was much inquired for.

The Queen Mother did not unmask, but in requital of some few ladies' and gentlemen's attendance there did vouchsafe to have the bate of the caroche put down and threw her vest upon it, where they and myself had the honour (if it may be called an honour) to salute the hem thereof . . .

DISSENSION DEVELOPS BETWEEN KING AND PEOPLE

THE FIVE KNIGHTS' CASE

A number of important people who refused to pay the forced loan to the King were imprisoned by his special command. Five of them, all knights, applied to the Court of King's Bench for a writ of habeas corpus, hoping to obtain their release. This is the judgment of Hyde, L.C.J., given on the 28th November 1627.

The next thing is the main point in law, whether the substance or matter of the return be good or no: wherein the substance is this — he [theWarden] doth certify that they are detained in prison by the special command of the King; and whether this be good in law or no, that is the question . . . [After examination of precedents] Then the precedents are all against you every one of them, and what shall guide our judgments, since there is nothing alleged in this case but precedents? That, if no cause of the commitment be expressed, it is to be presumed to be for matter of state, which we cannot take notice of; you see we find none, no, not one, that hath been delivered by bail in the like cases, but by the hand of the King or his direction . . . We have looked upon that precedent that was mentioned by Mr. Attorney — the resolution of all the judges of England in 34 Eliz. . . . The question now is, whether we may deliver these gentlemen or not . . . and this resolution of all the judges teacheth us; and what can we do but walk in the steps of our forefathers? . . . If in justice we ought to deliver you, we would do it; but upon these grounds and these records, and the precedents and resolutions, we cannot deliver you, but you must be remanded.

THE PETITION OF RIGHT
7th JUNE 1628

The Petition exhibited to His Majesty by the Lords Spiritual and Temporal, and Commons in this present Parliament assembled, concerning divers Rights and Liberties of the Subjects.

To the King's Most Excellent Majesty

Humbly show unto our Sovereign Lord the King, the Lords Spiritual and Temporal, and Commons in Parliament assembled, that whereas it is declared and enacted by a statute made in the time of the reign of King Edward the First, commonly called *Statutum de Tallagio non concedendo*, that no tallage or aid shall be laid or levied by the King or his heirs in this realm, without the goodwill and assent of the Archbishops, Bishops, Earls, Barons, Knights, Burgesses, and other the freemen of the commonalty of this realm: and by authority of Parliament holden in the five and twentieth year of the reign of King Edward the Third, it is declared and enacted, that from henceforth no person shall be compelled to make any loans to the King against his will . . . .

. . . .

Yet nevertheless, of late divers commissions directed to sundry Commissioners in several counties with instructions have issued, by means whereof your people have been in divers places assembled, and required to lend certain sums of money unto your Majesty, and many of them upon their refusal so to do . . . have been therefore imprisoned, confined, and sundry other ways molested and disquieted . . . .

And where also by the statute called, "The Great Charter of the Liberties of England", it is declared and enacted, that no freeman may be taken or imprisoned or be disseised of his freeholds or liberties, or his free customs, or be outlawed or exiled; or in any manner destroyed, but by the lawful judgment of his peers, or by the law of the land:

. . . .

Nevertheless, against the tenor of the said statutes, and other the good laws and statutes of your realm, to that end provided, divers of your subjects have of late been imprisoned without any cause showed, and when for their deliverance they were brought before your Justices, by your Majesty's writs of Habeas Corpus, there to undergo and receive as the Court should order, and their keepers commanded to certify the causes of their detainer; no cause was certified, but that they were detained by your Majesty's special command, signified by the Lords of your Privy Council, and yet were returned back to several prisons, without being charged with anything to which they might make answer according to the law:

And whereas of late great companies of soldiers and mariners have been dispersed into divers counties of the realm, and the inhabitants against their wills have been compelled to receive them into their houses, and there to suffer them to sojourn, against the laws and customs of this realm, and to the great grievance and vexation of the people:

. . . .

They do therefore humbly pray your Most Excellent Majesty, that no man hereafter be compelled to make or yield any gift, loan, benevolence, tax, or such like charge without common consent by Act of Parliament; and that none be called to make answer, or take such oath, or to give attendance, or be confined, or otherwise molested or disquieted concerning the same, or for refusal thereof; and that no freeman, in any such manner as is before-mentioned, be imprisoned or detained; and that your Majesty will be pleased to remove the said soldiers and mariners, and that your people may not be so burdened in time to come; . . . .

CHARLES I's SPEECH PROROGUING PARLIAMENT, 26th JUNE 1628

It may seem strange, that I come so suddenly to end this Session; wherefore before I give my assent to the Bills, I will tell you the cause, though I must avow, that I owe an account of my actions to none but to God alone. It is known to every one, that a while ago the House of Commons gave me a Remonstrance, how acceptable every man may judge; and for the merit of it, I will not call that in question, for I am sure no wise man can justify it.

Now since I am certainly informed, that a second Remonstrance is preparing for me to take away my profit of Tonnage and Poundage, one of the chief maintenances of my Crown, by alleging I have given away my right thereof by my answer to your Petition; this is so prejudicial unto me, that I am forced to end this Session some few hours before I meant it, being willing not to receive any more Remonstrances, to which I must give a harsh answer.

FIRST WRIT OF SHIP-MONEY
20th OCTOBER 1634

Ship-money was another dubiously legal device by which the King hoped to raise money.

Carolus Rex, etc.

To the Mayor, commonalty, and citizens of our city of London, and to the sheriffs of the same city, and good men in the said city and in the liberties, and members of the same, greeting: Because we are given to understand that certain thieves, pirates, and robbers of the sea, as well Turks, enemies of the Christian name, as others, being gathered together, wickedly taking by force and spoiling the ships, and goods, and merchandises, not only of our subjects, but also the subjects of our friends in the sea, which hath been accustomed anciently to be defended by the English nation, and the same, at their pleasure, have carried away, delivering the men in the same into miserable captivity: and forasmuch as we see them daily preparing all manner of shipping farther to molest our merchants, and to grieve the kingdom, unless remedy be not sooner applied, and their endeavours be not more manly met withal; also the dangers considered which, on every side, in these times of war do hang over our heads, that it behoveth us and our subjects to hasten the defence of the sea and kingdom with all expedition or speed that we can; we willing by the help of God chiefly to provide for the defence of the kingdom, safeguard of the sea, security of our subjects, safe conduct of ships and merchandises to our kingdom of England coming, and from the same kingdom to foreign parts passing; forasmuch as we, and our progenitors, Kings of England, have been always heretofore masters of the aforesaid sea and it would be very irksome unto us if that princely honour in our times should be lost or in any thing diminished . . . we command firmly, enjoining you the aforesaid Mayor, commonalty and citizens, and sheriffs of the said city, and the good men in the same city and in the liberties, and members of the same, in the faith and allegiance wherein you are bound unto us, and as you do love us and our honour, and under the forfeiture of all which you can forfeit to us, that you cause to be prepared and brought to the port of Portsmouth, before the first day of March now next ensuing, one ship of war of the burden of nine hundred tons, with three hundred and fifty men at the least, as well expert masters, as very able and skilful mariners; etc. . . . .

THE JUDGES' ANSWER CONCERNING THE KING'S RIGHT TO LEVY SHIP-MONEY
7th FEBRUARY 1637

May it please your Most Excellent Majesty,

We have, according to your Majesty's command, every man by himself, and all of us together, taken into serious consideration the case and question signed by your Majesty, and inclosed in your royal letter; and we are of opinion, that when the good and safety of the kingdom in general is concerned, and the kingdom in danger, your Majesty may, by writ under the Great Seal of England, command all your subjects of this your kingdom, at their charge to provide and furnish such a number of ships, with men, victuals, and munition, and for such time as your Majesty shall think fit for the defence and safeguard of this kingdom from such danger and peril: and that by law your Majesty may compel the doing thereof in case of refusal, or refractoriness: and we are also of opinion, that in such case your Majesty is the sole judge both of the danger, and when and how the same is to be prevented and avoided.

John Bramston	*George Croke*
John Finch	*Thomas Trevor*
Humphry Davenport	*George Vernon*
John Denham	*Francis Crawley*
Richard Hutton	*Robert Berkeley*
William Jones	*Richard Weston*

JOHN HAMPDEN

The Judges gave their answer about ship-money not following a trial, but in response to a question put to them by the King. Hampden, in the face of difficulty, managed to have the issue brought to trial. Finally judgment was given for the King, but two judges dissented and three others gave qualified opinions.

He was a gentleman of a good family in Buckinghamshire and born to a fair fortune, and of a most civil and affable deportment ... They who conversed nearly with him found him growing into a dislike of the ecclesiastical government of the Church, yet most believed it rather a dislike of some churchmen, and of some introducements of theirs which he apprehended might disquiet the public peace. He was rather of reputation in his own country [*i.e.* county] than of public discourse or fame in the Kingdom before the business of ship-money, but then he grew the argument of all tongues, every man enquiring who and what he was that durst at his own charge support the liberty and property of the Kingdom, and rescue his country from being under a prey to the Court . . . the judgment that was given against him infinitely more advanced him than the service for which it was given. When this Parliament began (being returned Knight of the Shire for the county where he lived) the eyes of all men were fixed upon him as their *Patriae Pater*, and the pilot that must steer their vessel through the tempests and rocks which threatened it. And I am persuaded his power and interest at that time was greater to do good or hurt than any man's in the Kingdom or than any man of his rank hath had at any time: for his reputation of honesty was universal, and his affections seemed so publicly guided that no corrupt or private ends could bias them.

He was of that rare affability and temper in debate, and of that seeming humility and submission of judgment, as if he brought no opinions with him, but a desire of information and instruction, yet he had so subtle a way of interrogating, and, under the notion of doubts, insinuating his objections, that he left his opinions with those from whom he pretended to learn and receive them . . . He was indeed a very wise man and of great parts, and possessed with the most absolute spirit of popularity, that is the most absolute faculties to govern the people, of any man I ever knew.

CLARENDON, *History of the Rebellion* (1646–71; pubd. 1702–4)

The charge of Lord Keeper Finch to the Judges in the Star Chamber, before going on circuit, 13th February 1640

. . . I know not how it comes about, I hope it is out of mis-apprehension and false intimation put into the hearts of his [the King's] people, but there is not [the] alacrity and cheerfulness given to the obedience of His Majesty's writs for ship-money that his affection and care of his people doth require . . .

ACT DECLARING SHIP-MONEY ILLEGAL
7th AUGUST 1641

. . . Be it therefore declared and enacted by the King's Most Excellent Majesty and the Lords and Commons in this present Parliament assembled, and by the authority of the same, that the said charge imposed upon the subject for the providing and furnishing of ships commonly called Ship-money, and the said extrajudicial opinion of the said Justices and Barons and the said writs, and every of them, and the said agreement or opinion of the greater part of the said Justices and Barons, and the said judgment given against the said John Hampden, were and are contrary to and against the laws and statutes of this realm, the right of property, the liberty of the subjects, former resolutions in Parliament, and the Petition of Right made in the third year of the reign of His Majesty that now is.

DISSENSION IN MATTERS OF RELIGION

REPUBLICATION OF JAMES I's DECLARATION OF SPORTS, 18th OCTOBER 1633

The republication of the Declaration was, and was intended to be, a blow to the increasingly important body of Puritans.

Our dear father of blessed memory, in his return from Scotland, coming through Lancashire, found that his subjects were debarred from lawful recreations upon Sundays after evening prayers ended, and upon Holy-days; and he prudently considered that, if these times were taken from them, the meaner sort who labour hard all the week should have no recreations at all to refresh their spirits; and after his return, he further saw that his loyal subjects in all other parts of his kingdom did suffer in the same kind, though perhaps not in the same degree; and did therefore in his princely wisdom publish a Declaration to all his loving subjects concerning lawful sports to be used at such times, which was printed and published by his royal commandment in the year 1618, in the tenor which hereafter followeth:

. . . .

Our express pleasure therefore is that no lawful recreation shall be barred to our good people, which shall not tend to the breach of our aforesaid laws and canons of our Church: which to express more particularly, our pleasure is, that the Bishop, and all other inferior churchmen and churchwardens, shall for their parts be careful and diligent, both to instruct the ignorant, and convince and reform them that are misled in religion,

17

presenting them that will not conform themselves, but obstinately stand out, to our Judges and Justices: whom we likewise command to put the law in due execution against them. ... and as for our good people's lawful recreation, our pleasure likewise is, that after the end of divine service our good people be not disturbed, letted or discouraged from any lawful recreation, such as dancing, either men or women; archery for men, leaping, vaulting, or any other such harmless recreation, nor from having of May-games, Whitsun-ales, and Morris-dances; and the setting up of May-poles and other sports therewith used: so as the same be had in due and convenient time, without impediment or neglect of divine service: and that women shall have leave to carry rushes to the church for the decorating of it, according to their old custom; but withal we do here account still as prohibited all unlawful games to be used upon Sundays only, as bear and bull-baitings, interludes and at all times in the meaner sort of people by law prohibited, bowling.

. . . .

Now out of a like pious care for the service of God, and for suppressing of any humours that oppose truth, and for the ease, comfort and recreation of our well-deserving people, His Majesty doth ratify and publish this our blessed father's Declaration . .
. . . . . .

Given at our Palace of Westminster, the eighteenth day of October, in the ninth year of our Reign.

God save the King.

ORDINANCE OF PARLIAMENT, 5th MAY 1643

It is this day ordered by the Lords and Commons in Parliament, that the Book concerning the enjoining and tolerating of sports upon the Lord's Day be forthwith burned by the hand of the Common Hang-man in Cheapside and other usual places.

JUDGMENT OF THE COURT OF STAR CHAMBER AGAINST WILLIAM PRYNNE, 1634

Prynne, a copious and phrenetic writer and at this time with strong Puritan leanings, published in 1633 Histriomastix, or a Scourge for Stage Players *in which he attacked with particular ferocity plays in which women took part — as the Queen had done at Court. He was brought before the Star Chamber for criminal libel, the only court which could then try that offence.*

Mr. Prynne hath printed a book against the whole Kingdom, against the best sort of mankind, as Kings, Queens, and Princes; I cannot tell whether he assisted the devil or the devil assisted him in the doing it. There is matter in it against our Saviour himself. Mr. Prynne dislikes masques and dancing, yet he answers one thing and swears another. He answers that the former book, showed to Dr. Goad and Dr. Harris was part of it, but he swears to the contrary. The truth is Mr. Prynne would have a new Government, a new Church, a new King, new laws, and all the people discontented. He confesseth that he wrote this scandalous book; now by his words and acts he shall be judged. And as all good men receive part in the scandal, so let all good men delight in his punishment. This scandal proceeds not from the mouth of some poor rogue but from one that maintains it by authors and arguments, very horrid things. He speaks positively that the English ladies have lost all modesty and nature, religion and honesty, etc.; that frequenters of plays are all damned, that all that do not concur in his opinions are devils incarnate: these are horrid things. He hath had more time in this Court for trial [four days] than I ever knew any in the like kind. I will now fall to sentence and do him right:

1. First the books are to be burnt in the basest manner by the hand of the hangman.
2. For Mr. Prynne, I would have him put from the Bar, from the profession of the Law.

3. Disfranchised from the Society of Lincoln's Inn.

4. Degraded in the University [Oxford].

5. To stand in the pillory in the two usual places, Westminster and Cheapside, and to have his ears cut off; with a paper in his hat as a seditious person.

6. Fined at 5000 li. to the King.

7. Imprisonment perpetual, or at the King's pleasure.

[It is not certain when Prynne was freed from prison, but within the next two years he wrote and published four more books, the fourth of which, *Newes from Ipswich*, again got him into trouble with the Star Chamber. His previous sentence was repeated — a £5000 fine, the pillory, and to have his ears cut off, again.]

He [William Prynne] was a learned man, of immense reading, but is much blamed for his unfaithful quotations. His manner of study was thus: he wore a long quilt cap, which came two or three, at least, inches over his eyes, which served him as an umbrella to defend his eyes from the light. About every three hours his man was to bring him a roll and a pot of ale to refocillate his wasted spirits . . . So he studied and drank and munched some bread; and this maintained him 'till night; and then he made a good supper. Now he did well not to dine, which breaks off one's fancy, which will not presently be regained: and 'tis with invention as a flux — when once it is flowing it runs amain; if it is checked, flows but *guttim*: and the like for perspiration — check it, and 'tis spoiled.

JOHN AUBREY (1626–97), *Brief Lives*

A WARRANT OF THE COURT OF HIGH COMMISSION

The Court of High Commission was established following the Reformation to regulate the affairs of the Church in England. It was much used by Archbishop Laud in his attempts to tighten up ecclesiastical discipline, and became exceedingly objectionable to the Puritans, and therefore to Parliament.

These are to will and require you in His Majesty's name by virtue of His Highness' commission for causes ecclesiastical under the Great Seal of England to us and others directed, that taking with you a constable and such other assistance as you shall think meet, you do forthwith upon the receipt thereof enter into the house of John Fennar of Egerton in the county of Kent, pail-maker or carpenter (who is a known dangerous schismatical recusant) and therein and every room and place thereof do make diligent search for all manner of unlawful, seditious, or prohibited books, pamphlets, libels, or writings, wheresoever they may be found, as well in places exempt as not exempt, and the same, or any such so found, to seize into your hands and to detain under sure and safe custody, and bring them forthwith before us or others our colleagues to be examined, viewed, and disposed of as shall be thought meet or agreeable to justice, but howsoever his books, papers, and writings may be conveyed away or concealed, yet nevertheless we will and require you in His Majesty's name by authority aforesaid forthwith upon the receipt hereof to apprehend and attach or cause to be apprehended and attached the said John Fennar wheresoever he may be found, as well in places exempt as not exempt, and that thereupon you do detain him under safe custody and bring or send him forthwith before us . . . to answer unto such matters as on His Majesty's behalf shall be objected against him and to receive such further direction therein as to justice shall appertain . . .

Given at Lambeth this 26th of January 1635 [1636]

W. Cant.

Jo. Lambe
Na. Brent.

WILLIAM LAUD

He was a man of great parts and very exemplar virtues, allayed and discredited by some unpopular natural infirmities. He was always maligned and persecuted by those who were of the Calvinian faction, which was then very powerful, and who according to their useful maxim and practice call every man they do not love, Papist, and under this senseless appellation they created him many troubles and vexations . . . When he came into authority it may be he retained too keen a memory of those who had so unjustly and uncharitably persecuted him before, and I doubt was so far transported with the same passions he had reason to complain of in his adversaries, that, as they accused him of Popery, because he had some doctrinal opinions which they liked not — though they were nothing allied to Popery — so he entertained too much prejudice to some persons, as if they were enemies to the discipline of the Church, because they concurred with Calvin in some doctrinal points, when they abhorred his discipline and reverenced the government of the Church, and prayed for the peace of it, with as much zeal and fervency as any in the Kingdom . . .

He was a man of great courage and resolution, and being most assured within himself that he proposed no end in all his actions and designs than what was pious and just (as sure no man ever had a heart more entire to the King, the Church or his country) he never studied the best ways to those ends . . .

He intended the discipline of the Church should be felt as well as spoken of, and that it should be applied to the greatest and most splendid transgressors . . . persons of honour and great quality, of the Court, were every day cited into the High Commission Court, upon the fame of their incontinence or other scandal in their lives; and were there prosecuted to their shame and punishment, and the shame (which they called an insolent triumph upon their degree and quality and levelling them with the common people) was never forgotten, but watched for revenge . . .

CLARENDON, *History of the Rebellion* (1646–71; pubd. 1702–4)

... As this good Archbishop I write of had these great eminences, so he may be acknowledged to have failed in those prudences which belong unto a great Minister of State, who like a wise physician is to consider times and seasons as well as persons and diseases.

SIR PHILIP WARWICK (1609–83), *Memoirs* (pubd. 1701)

PARLIAMENT, 1640–2

For eleven years Charles had ruled without a Parliament. The news that he was summoning his fourth Parliament in the Spring of 1640 was received with relief and high hopes, for men believed that it would reduce the mounting tensions within the Kingdom. But after three weeks Charles dissolved it, for it insisted on discussing the subjects' grievances before the King's financial needs. In November 1640 Parliament had to be summoned again, and sat on (or some of it did) until 1653 — the Long Parliament.

Theophilus Higgens to Sir Roger Twysden, M.P.,
30th March 1640
. . . The ship-money business is the matter most likely to produce some ill in this Parliament if it be not managed with singular wisdom. The more ingenious sort of the countrymen do verily consider that the King, in case of necessity, may impose it, and that he is the most proper judge of the necessity.
Four things do trouble them:

1. that a necessity may be pretended against the laws and approved customs of the Kingdom wherefore they wish that the Necessity were particularly explained and agreed upon between His Majesty and his people for the time to come.
2. that the moneys collected on the pretence of a necessity may be used for another purpose . . .
3. the extent of the ship-money may be enlarged at the Prince's pleasure and grow into an unsupportable burden . . .
4. the farmers do complain bitterly of inequalities in the imposition of the charge . . .

I hope that you and all the other worshipful discreet gentlemen
will sweeten all things to your power and not provoke His Majesty
and that by fair treaty and entreaty things may be reduced to a
good and peaceable conclusion. This is to be called The Happy or
The Unhappy Parliament. [In fact it was known as The Short
Parliament.]

JOHN PYM

. . . He had been well known in former Parliaments and was one
of those few who had sat in many, the long intermission of Parliaments having worn out most of those who had been acquainted
with the rules and orders observed in those conventions, and this
gave him some reputation and reverence amongst those who were
but now introduced. He had been most taken notice of for being
concerned and passionate in the jealousies of religion . . . and this
gave him great authority and interest with those who were pleased
with the Government of the Church or the growing power of the
clergy, yet himself industriously took care to be believed, and he
professed to be, very entire to the doctrine and discipline of the
Church of England. In the Short Parliament before this, he spake
much and appeared to be the most leading man, for besides the
exact knowledge of the forms and orders of that council, which
few men had, he had a very comely and grave way of expressing
himself, with great volubility of words, natural and proper, and
understood the temper and affections of the Kingdom as well as
any man, and had observed the errors and mistakes in government
and knew well how to make them appear greater than they were . . .
    At the first opening of this Parliament [the Long Parliament]
he appeared passionate and prepared against the Earl of Strafford,
and though in private designing he was much governed by Mr.
Hampden and Mr. St. John, yet he seemed to all men to have the
greatest influence upon the House of Commons of any man . . .
In the prosecution of the Earl of Strafford his carriage and language

was such that expressed much personal animosity, and he was accused of having practised some arts in it not worthy of a good man; as an Irishman of very mean and low condition afterwards acknowledged, that being brought to him as an evidence of one part of the charge against the Lord Lieutenant in a particular of which a person of so vile quality would not reasonably be thought a competent informer, Mr. Pym gave him money to buy him a satin suit and cloak, in which equipage he appeared at the trial and gave his evidence; which, if true, may make many other things which were confidently reported afterwards of him to be believed . . .

From the time of his being accused of high treason by the King, with the Lord Kimbolton and the other Members, he never entertained thoughts of moderation, but always opposed all overtures of peace and accommodation.

During his sickness he was a very sad spectacle, but none being admitted to him who had not concurred with him, it is not known what his last thoughts and considerations were. He died towards the end of December [1643] and was buried with wonderful pomp and magnificence in that place where the bones of our English Kings and Princes are committed to their rest.

CLARENDON, History of the Rebellion (1646–71;
pubd. 1702–4)

CROMWELL AND THE LONG PARLIAMENT

I have no mind to give an ill character of Cromwell; for in his conversation towards me he was ever friendly . . . The first time that I ever took notice of him was in the very beginning of the Parliament held in November, 1640, when I vainly thought myself a courtly young gentleman (for we courtiers valued ourselves much upon our good clothes). I came one morning into the house well clad, and perceived a gentleman speaking (whom I knew not) very ordinarily apparelled; for it was a plain cloth-suit, which seemed to have been made by an ill country-tailor; his linen was plain and not very clean . . . his countenance swollen and reddish, his voice sharp and untunable, and his eloquence full of fervour . . . And yet I lived to see this very gentleman, whom out of no ill will to him I thus describe, by multiplied good successes and by real (but usurped) power (having had a better tailor and more converse among good company) . . . appear of a great and majestic deportment and comely presence. Of him therefore I will say no more, but that verily I believe he was extraordinarily designed for those extraordinary things, which one while most wickedly and facinorously he acted, and at another as successfully and greatly performed.

SIR PHILIP WARWICK (1609–83), *Memoirs* (pubd. 1701)

Oliver Cromwell, to Mrs. St. John, 13th October 1638

. . . Truly no poor creature has more cause to put himself forth in the cause of his God than I. I have had plentiful wages beforehand, and I am sure I shall never earn the least mite. The Lord accept me in His Son, and to give me to walk in the light . . . I dare not say, He hideth his face from me. He giveth me to see light in His light— blessed be His name for shining upon so dark a heart as mine. You know what my manner of life hath been. Oh, I lived in and loved darkness, and hated light; I was a chief, the chief of sinners. This is true: I hated Godliness, yet God had mercy on me. Oh, the riches of His mercy. Praise Him for me! . . .

THE ROOT AND BRANCH PETITION
11th DECEMBER 1640

To the Right Honourable the Commons Houses of Parliament.

The humble Petition of many of His Majesty's subjects in and about the City of London, and several Counties of the Kingdom.

Sheweth,

That whereas the government of archbishops and lord bishops, deans and archdeacons, &c., with their courts and ministrations in them, have proved prejudicial and very dangerous both to the Church and Commonwealth, they themselves having formerly held that they have their jurisdiction or authority of human authority, till of these later times, being further pressed about the unlawfulness, that they have claimed their calling immediately from the Lord Jesus Christ, which is against the laws of this kingdom, and derogatory to His Majesty and his state royal. And whereas the said government is found by woeful experience to be a main cause and occasion of many foul evils, pressures and grievances of a very high nature unto His Majesty's subjects in their own consciences, liberties and estates, as in a schedule of particulars hereunto annexed may in part appear:

We therefore most humbly pray, and beseech this honourable assembly, the premises considered, that the said government, with all its dependencies, roots and branches, may be abolished, and all laws in their behalf made void, and the government according to God's Word may be rightly placed amongst us: and we your humble suppliants, as in duty we are bound, will daily pray for His Majesty's long and happy reign over us, and for the prosperous success of this high and honourable Court of Parliament.

Following the Root and Branch Petition, Sir Edward Dering introduced into the Commons a Bill for the utter extirpation of the episcopacy.

Edward Kempe to Sir Edward Dering, M.P., 15th December 1640

'Tis since reported by some small divines about the Cathedral [Canterbury] that you have been dangerously sick in mind (in plain terms mad) otherwise you would never have uttered such things as you have done in Parliament . . . I beseech God bless your labours and give good success to it; 'tis the prayers, I hope, of all good men.

Numerous Puritan petitions were submitted to Parliament in 1640 and 1641 complaining about the Church service ceremonies insisted on by Archbishop Laud. The following examples come from Kent parishes. As the withdrawal of the Snargate complaint shows, unjustified petitions were sometimes got up by a small group of parishioners in the heat of the moment.

Minster-in-Thanet against the Rev. Dr. Meric Casaubon. He and his curate "are zealously observant of all innovations, as bowing and cringing to the communion table."

East Peckham against the Rev. Francis Worrall. "... that the communion table is set up at the east end of the chancel, close to the wall, altar-wise and railed in, and a new wainscot made behind it with the picture of angels carved therein ..."

Horsmonden against the Rev. Jeffrey Amherst. "... He continually boweth at the name of Jesus, and presseth his people to observe new gestures in the church ..."

Snargate, 7th April, 1641. "Whereas of late, by the instigation of a malignant humour, being too precipitate in preferring certain articles against our curate Mr. John Freeman ... we confess him to be both very able, sufficient, and painful in dispensing the word of God: but only he seemed to carry himself somewhat too lofty, and to be hasty towards us."

The following extract gives a taste of the Puritan enthusiasm, buoyed up with hopes of an early coming of the Millenium, which engendered some of the petitions against the parochial clergy.

... It is the work of the day to cry down Babylon, that it may fall more and more; and it is the work of the day to give God no rest till he sets up Jerusalem as the praise of the whole world. Blessed

is he that dasheth the brats of Babylon against the stones. Blessed
is he that hath any hand in pulling down Babylon . . .

But when shall these things be? Truly, brethren, we hope it is
not long before they shall be . . . No place in scripture gives us so
much light to know when this shall be as Dan. xii. 11 . . . Now
reckon so many years according to the number of days, it comes to
1650; and it is now 1641 . . .

KNOLLYS, *A Glimpse of Sion's Glory* (1641)

THE ECONOMIC CONSEQUENCES OF THE DISTURBANCES

Petition of divers citizens of London to the Honourable Assembly
of the Lords and Commons, 24th April 1641

Sheweth . . .

As the unsettled condition of the Kingdom, ever since the
troubles in Scotland, hath caused both strangers and also some of
our own, who did furnish great sums of money to use, to call it in
and remit much of it by exchange into foreign parts . . .

The stopping-money in the Mint, which till then was accounted
the safest place and surest staple in these parts of the World, still doth
hinder the importation of Bullion . . .

The English trade, by reason of our general distractions and fears,
is so much decayed that country tradesmen cannot pay their debts
in London as formerly . . .

Subscribed by 20,000 persons of good rank and quality.

ACT ATTAINTING THE EARL OF STRAFFORD,
10th MAY 1641

Strafford, with his watchword of "Thorough", was the King's principal agent in secular affairs as Laud was in ecclesiastical. Both became obnoxious to the Commons, and both were beheaded, Strafford in 1641 and Laud four years later. The Bill attainting Strafford passed the third reading by 204 to 59 votes.

Be it therefore enacted by the King's Most Excellent Majesty, and by the Lords and Commons in this present Parliament assembled and by authority of the same, that the said Earl of Strafford, for the heinous crimes and offences aforesaid stand and be adjudged and attainted of high treason, and shall suffer such pains of death, and incur the forfeitures of his goods and chattels, lands, tenements and hereditaments of any estate of freehold or inheritance in the said kingdoms of England and Ireland, which the said Earl or any other to his use, or in trust for him, have or had, the day of the first sitting of this Parliament, or at any time since.

THE EXECUTION OF STRAFFORD

All things being thus transacted to conclude the fate of this great person, he was on the 12 day of May [1641] brought from the Tower of London where he had been a prisoner near six months to the scaffold on Tower Hill, where with a composed, undaunted courage he told the people, he was come thither to satisfy them with his head, but that he much feared the reformation which was begun in blood would not prove so fortunate to the Kingdom as they expected and he wished, and after great expressions of his devotion to the Church of England and the Protestant Religion established by Law and professed in that Church, of his loyalty to the King and affection to the peace and welfare of the Kingdom, with marvellous tranquility of mind, he delivered his head to the block, where it was severed from his body at a blow; many of the standers by, who had not been over charitable to him in his life, being much affected with the courage and Christianity of his death.

CLARENDON, *History of the Rebellion* (1646–71; pubd. 1702–4)

THE CHARACTER OF STRAFFORD

. . . He was every way qualified for business, his natural faculties being very strong and pregnant, his understanding, aided by a good fancy, made him quick in discerning the nature of any business; and through a cold brain he became deliberate and of a sound judgment. His memory was great, and he made it greater by confiding in it. His elocution was very fluent and it was a great part of his talent readily to reply, or freely to harangue, upon any subject. And all this was lodged in a sour and haughty temper; so as it may probably be believed he expected to have more observance paid to him than he was willing to pay to others, though they were of his own quality; and then he was not like to conciliate the good will of men of the lesser station.

His acquired parts, both in University and Inns-of-Court learning, as likewise his foreign travels, made him an eminent man before he was a conspicuous . . . As he had those parts he knew how to set a price on them, if not overvalue them: and he too soon discovered a roughness in his nature, which a man no more obliged by him than I was would have called an injustice; though many of his confidants . . . were wont to swear to me that he endeavoured to be just to all, but was resolved to be gracious to none but to those whom he inwardly thought affected him: which never bowed me till his broken fortune and, as I thought, very unjustifiable prosecution made me one of the fifty-six who gave a negative to that fatal Bill which cut the thread of his life.

SIR PHILIP WARWICK (1609–83), *Memoirs* (pubd. 1701)

ACT AGAINST DISSOLVING THE LONG PARLIAMENT, 10th MAY 1641

Parliament was determined not again to be dissolved abruptly by the King, and so prolonged its life indefinitely.

And be it declared and enacted by the King, our Sovereign Lord, with the assent of the Lords and Commons in this present Parliament assembled, and by the authority of the same, that this present Parliament now assembled shall not be dissolved unless it be by Act of Parliament to be passed for that purpose; . . . .

ACT ABOLISHING THE COURT OF STAR CHAMBER, 5th JULY 1641

The Court of Star Chamber was by no means merely an instrument of oppression. It was a useful part of the machinery of administration and of justice, but it was unpopular because it was an aspect of the King's prerogative, it sometimes acted arbitrarily, and it was uncontrollable by the Common Law Courts. The Court of High Commission was likewise abolished, with the consequence, its supporters said, that vice flourished more abundantly.

. . . and forasmuch as all matters examinable or determinable before the said Judges, or in the Court commonly called the Star Chamber, may have their proper remedy and redress, and their due punishment and correction by the common law of the land, and in the ordinary course of justice elsewhere, and forasmuch as the reasons and motives inducing the erection and continuance of that Court do now cease, and the proceedings, censures and decrees of that Court have by experience been found to be an intolerable burden to the subjects, and the means to introduce an arbitrary power and government; . . . . for settling whereof and preventing the like in time to come, be it ordained and enacted by the authority of this present Parliament, that the said Court commonly called the Star Chamber, and all jurisdiction, power and authority belonging unto or exercised in the same Court, or by any of the Judges, Officers or Ministers thereof be, from the first day of August in the year of our Lord God one thousand six hundred forty and one, clearly and absolutely dissolved, taken away, and determined; . . . . . .

PETITION ACCOMPANYING THE GRAND REMONSTRANCE OF THE HOUSE OF COMMONS TO THE KING, 1st DECEMBER 1641

. . . we have been necessitated to make a declaration of the state of the kingdom, both before and since the assembly of this Parliament, unto this time, which we do humbly present to your Majesty, without the least intention to lay any blemish upon your royal person, but only to represent how your royal authority and trust have been abused, to the great prejudice and danger of your Majesty, and of all your good subjects.

And because we have reason to believe that those malignant parties, whose proceedings evidently appear to be mainly for the advantage and increase of Popery, is composed, set up, and acted by the subtile practice of the Jesuits and other engineers and factors for Rome, and to the great danger of this kingdom, and most grievous affliction of your loyal subjects, have so far prevailed as to corrupt divers of your Bishops and others in prime places of the Church, and also to bring divers of these instruments to be of your Privy Council, and other employments of trust and nearness about your Majesty, the Prince, and the rest of your royal children.

And by this means have had such an operation in your counsel and the most important affairs and proceedings of your government, that a most dangerous division and chargeable preparation for war betwixt your kingdoms of England and Scotland, the increase of jealousies betwixt your Majesty and your most obedient subjects, the violent distraction and interruption of this Parliament, the insurrection of the Papists in your kingdom of Ireland, and bloody massacre of your people, have been not only endeavoured and attempted, but in a great measure compassed and effected.

For preventing the final accomplishment whereof, your poor subjects are enforced to engage their persons and estates to the maintaining of a very expensive and dangerous war [in Ireland], notwithstanding they have already since the beginning of this Parliament undergone the charge of £150,000 sterling, or thereabouts, for the necessary support and supply of your Majesty in these present and perilous designs. And because all our most faithful endeavours and engagements will be ineffectual for the peace, safety and preservation of your Majesty and your people, if some present, real and effectual course be not taken for suppressing this wicked and malignant party:—

We, your most humble and obedient subjects, do with all faithfulness and humility beseech your Majesty —

1. That you will be graciously pleased to concur with the humble desires of your people in a parliamentary way, for the preserving the peace and safety of the kingdom from the malicious designs of the Popish party:—

   For depriving the Bishops of their votes in Parliament, and abridging their immoderate power usurped over the Clergy, and other your good subjects, which they have perniciously abused to the hazard of religion, and great prejudice and oppression to the laws of the kingdom, and just liberty of your people:—

   For the taking away such oppressions in religion, Church government and discipline, as have been brought in and fomented by them:—

   For uniting all such your loyal subjects together as join in the same fundamental truths against the Papists, by removing some oppressive and unnecessary ceremonies by which divers weak consciences have been scrupled, and seem to be divided from the rest, and for the due execution of those good laws which have been made for securing the liberty of your subjects.

2. That your Majesty will likewise be pleased to remove from your council all such as persist to favour and promote any of those pressures and corruptions wherewith your people have been grieved; and that for the future your Majesty will vouchsafe to employ such persons in your great and public affairs, and to take such to be near you in places of trust, as your Parliament may have cause to confide in; that in your princely goodness to your people you will reject and refuse all mediation and solicitation to the contrary, how powerful and near soever.

3. That you will be pleased to forbear to alienate any of the aforfeited and escheated lands in Ireland which shall accrue to your Crown by reason of this rebellion, that out of them the Crown may be the better supported, and some satisfaction made to your subjects of this kingdom for the great expenses they are like to undergo [in] this war.

PREAMBLE TO THE KING'S ANSWER TO THE PETITION, 23rd DECEMBER 1641

We having received from you, soon after our return out of Scotland, a long petition consisting of many desires of great moment, together with a declaration of a very unusual nature annexed thereunto, we had taken some time to consider of it, as befitted us in a matter of that consequence, being confident that your own reason and regard to us, as well as our express intimation by our Comptroller, to that purpose, would have restrained you from the publishing of it till such time as you should have received our answer to it; but, much against our expectation, finding the contrary, that the said declaration is already abroad in print, by directions from your House as appears by the printed copy, we must let you know that we are very sensible of the disrespect. Notwithstanding, it is our intention that no failing on your part shall make us fail in ours of giving all due satisfaction to the desires of our people in a parliamentary way; and therefore we send you this answer to your petition, reserving ourself in point of the declaration which we think unparliamentary, and shall take a course to do that which we shall think fit in prudence and honour.

ATTEMPTED ARREST OF THE FIVE MEMBERS
4th JANUARY 1642

Charles determined to carry the war into the enemy's camp by accusing Pym, Hampden, Holles, Hazelrig and Strode, five leading M.P.s, of treason. Urged on by the Queen "to pull out the rogues by the ears", Charles went to the House of Commons to make the arrest himself, but, warned of his coming, the five members had taken refuge in the City of London.

. . . the King came with all his guard and all his pensioners, and two or three hundred soldiers and gentlemen. The King commanded the soldiers to stay in the Hall and sent us word he was at the door . . . the King came to the door and took the Palsgrave [his nephew] in with him and command[ed] all that came with him, upon their lives, not to come in . . . Then the King came upwards, towards the Chair, with his hat off, and the Speaker stepped out to meet him. Then the King stepped up to his place and stood upon the step but sat not down in the Chair. And, after he had looked a great while, he told us he would not break our privileges, but treason had no privilege; he came for those five gentlemen . . . Then he called Mr. Pym and Mr. Holles by name, but no answer was made. Then he asked the Speaker if they were here, or where they were. Upon that the Speaker fell on his knees and desired his excuse, for he was a servant to the House and had neither eyes nor tongue to see or say anything but what they commanded him. Then the King told him, he thought his own eyes as good as his, and then said, The birds were flown, but he did expect the House would send them to him, and if they did not he would seek them for himself, for their treason was foul and such an one as they would all thank him to discover. Then he assured us they shall all have a fair trial, and so went out, putting off his hat till he came to the door.

Sir Ralph Verney's note-book.

A DECLARATION OF THE HOUSE OF COMMONS TOUCHING A LATE BREACH OF THEIR PRIVILEGES 17th JANUARY 1642

And whereas, upon several examinations taken the 7th day of this instant January, before the committee appointed by the House of Commons to sit in London, it did fully appear that many soldiers, Papists and others, to the number of about five hundred, came with His Majesty on Tuesday last to the said House of Commons, armed with swords, pistols and other weapons, and divers of them pressed to the door of the said House, thrust away the door-keepers, and placed themselves between the said door and the ordinary attendants of His Majesty, holding up their swords, and some holding up their pistols ready cocked near the said door and saying, "I am a good marksman; I can hit right, I warrant you", and they not suffering the said door according to the custom of Parliament to be shut, but said they would have the door open, and if any opposition were against them, they made no question but they should make their party good, and that they would maintain their party; and when several members of the House of Commons were coming into the House, their attendants desiring that room might be made for them, some of the said soldiers answered, "A pox of God confound them", and others said, "A pox take the House of Commons, let them come and be hanged, what ado is here with the House of Commons?" And some of the said soldiers did likewise violently assault, and by force disarm some of the attendants and servants of the members of the House of Commons waiting in the room next the said House, and upon the King's return out of the said House, many of them by wicked oaths and otherwise, expressed much discontent that some members of the said House for whom they came were not there, and others of them said, " When comes the word?" And no word being given, at His Majesty's coming out they cried, "A lane, a lane"; afterwards some of them being demanded what they thought the said company intended to have done, answered that, questionless, in the posture they were set, if the word had been given, they should have fallen upon the House of Commons and have cut all their throats. Upon all which we are of opinion, that it is sufficiently proved that the coming of the said soldiers, Papists and others, with His Majesty to the House of Commons on Tuesday last, being the 4th of this instant January, in the manner aforesaid, was to take away some of the members of the said House; and if they should have found opposition or denial, then to have fallen upon the said House in an hostile manner. And we do hereby declare, that the same was a traitorous design against the King and Parliament . . . . .

THE KENTISH PETITION, MARCH 1642

Parliament was now constantly receiving petitions. This one, with its strong support of the Established Church, was drafted by a group of Kentish gentlemen at the March 1642 Assizes. It epitomises the things which were in debate: religion, the problem of Ireland, control of the militia, the powers of the two Houses of Parliament, the national revenue, trade, the safety of the realm, even the balance-of-payments problem. Clause 8 came in by accident — there happened to be a Doctor of Civil Law in court when the petition was under discussion. Parliament heard about it, suppressed it, and imprisoned the four men who were most active in getting it up. A few weeks later Richard Lovelace (see p. 93) made another attempt to deliver the petition; he, too, was imprisoned.

To the honourable House of Commons,

The humble petition of the gentry, ministry and commonalty of the county of Kent agreed upon at the general Assizes for that county

Most humbly sheweth

That we cannot but take notice how welcome to this honourable House many petitions have been, which yet came not from an assembled body of any county as this doth, we do hope to find as gentle and as favourable receptions of this, as any others have found of their petitions, our hearts witnessing unto us as good, as peaceable and as pious purposes as the best. These are therefore the true and the ardent desires of this county.

1. First, that you will please to accept our due and hearty thanks for those excellent laws, which by his Majesty's grace and goodness, you have obtained for us.

2. Secondly, that all laws against papists be put in due execution and account taken of their disarming, and that all children of papists may be brought up in the reformed religion.

3. Thirdly, that the solemn liturgy of the church of England, celebrious by the piety of holy bishops and martyrs who composed it, established by the supreme law of this land, attested and approved by the best of all foreign divines, confirmed with subscription of all the ministry of this land, a clergy as learned and as able as any in the Christian world, enjoyed and with an holy love embraced by the most and best of all the laity, that this holy exercise of our religion, may by your authority be enjoyed, quiet and free from interruptions, scorns, profanations, threats and force of such men, who daily do deprave it, and neglect the use of it in divers churches, in despite of the laws established.

4. Fourthly that episcopal government, as ancient in this island as Christianity itself, deduced and dispersed throughout the Christian world, even from the apostolical time, may be preserved as the most pious, most prudent and most safe government for the peace of the Church.

5. Fifthly, that all differences concerning religion and ceremonies may be referred to a lawful free national Synod and as your Remonstrance promiseth a general Synod of most grave, pious, learned and judicious divines, the proper agents, whose interest gifts and callings may quicken them in that great work, whose choice to be by all the clergy of the land, because all the clergy are to be bound by their resolutions and the determinations of this Synod to bind us all, when you have first formed them into a law, and this we take to be according to the ancient fundamental laws of this land confirmed by Magna Carta.

6. Sixthly, that some speedy and good provision may be made, as by his Majesty hath been, and is by all good men desired, against the odious and abominable scandal of schismatical and seditious sermons and pamphlets and some severe law made against lay men, for daring to arrogate to themselves and to exercise the holy function of the ministry, who, some of them, do sow their impious discontented doctrines even in sacred places, by abuse of sacred ordinances, to the advancing of heresy, schism, profaneness, libertinism, anabaptism, atheism.

7. Seventhly, that if the coercive power of ecclesiastical courts, by way of excommunication, be already abrogated, or shall be thought fit so to be, that there be some other power and authority speedily established, for the suppressing of the heinous and now so much abounding sins of incest, adultery, fornication and other crimes and for the recovering of tithes, repairing of churches, probates of wills, church assesses and providing of bread and wine for the Communion and choice of church-wardens, and other officers in the Church and especially for ministers who neglect the celebrating of Holy Communion and of parishioners for not receiving.

8. Eighthly, that the professors of that learned faculty of the civil law, without which this kingdom cannot but suffer many inconveniences, may not find discouragement and so desert their studies and professions.

9. Ninthly, that honour and profit, the powerful encouragements of industry, learning and piety, may be preserved without any farther diminution to the clergy.

10. Tenthly, that you please sadly to consider the bleeding wounds of our brethren in Ireland and with speedy succours endeavour to preserve them, whereunto his Majesty hath promised a gracious concurrence.

11. Eleventh, that you please to frame an especial law for the regulating the militia of this kingdom, so that the subjects may know how at once to obey both his Majesty and the Houses of Parliament, a law whereby may be left to the discretion of governors as little as may be, but that the number of arms and what measure of punishment shall be inflicted on offenders may be expressly set down in the Act, and not left to any arbitrary power, and that according to the precedent of former laws, the offenders may not be tried out of the county.

12. Twelfth, that the precious liberty of the subject, the common birthright of every Englishman, may be as in all other points preserved entire, so in this also, that no order of either or both Houses not grounded on the laws of the land may be enforced on the subject, until it be fully enacted by Parliament.

13. Thirteenth, that his Majesty's gracious message of the 20th of January last for the present and future establishment of the privilege of Parliament, the free and quiet enjoying of our estates, and fortunes, the liberties of our persons, the security of the true religion professed, the maintaining of his Majesty's just and regal authority, the establishing of his revenue, may be taken into speedy consideration, the effecting whereof will satisfy the desires of all us, his faithful and loving subjects.

14. Fourteenth, that all possible care may be taken that the native commodities of this kingdom may have a quick vent and that clothing and other manufactures may be improved, wherein the livelihood of many thousands do

consist and that trade may be so balanced that the importation do not exceed the exportation, which otherwise will in time prove the consumption of the kingdom.

15. Fifteenth, that you please to frame up some laws, concerning depopulations, purveyance, cart-taking, delays in justice, traffic, fishing on the coast, fulling earth, that our sea forts may be repaired and our magazines renewed.

16. Sixteenth, that you please to consider the general poverty that seems to overgrow the land.

17. Lastly, we humbly beseech you to consider, the sad condition that we and the whole land are in, if a good understanding be not speedily renewed, between his Majesty and the Houses of Parliament.

DRIFTING INTO WAR

Henry Oxinden of Deane, from London, to Henry Oxinden of Barham, 27th January 1642

. . . The great expectation that is now is the King's answer, which will produce some great effect one way or other; trade being stopped, the poor of [the] city are daily feared to rise, and also of other parts of the Kingdom. I find all here full of fears and almost void of hopes. Parents and children, brothers, kindred, ay, and dear friends have the seed of difference and division abundantly sowed in them. Sometimes I meet with a cluster of gentlemen equally divided in opinion and resolution, sometimes three to two, sometimes more odds, but never unanimous, nay more, I have heard foul language and desperate quarrelings even between old and entire friends, and how we can stand thus and not fall, certainly God must needs work a miracle parallel to some of his great ones in the old time. I am glad you have got a horse; provide you of arms; it is Mars, not Venus, that now can help . . .

THE MILITIA ORDINANCE, 5th MARCH 1642;
THE STRUGGLE FOR CONTROL

An Ordinance of the Lords and Commons in Parliament, for the safety and defence of the kingdom of England and dominion of Wales.

Whereas there hath been of late a most dangerous and desperate design upon the House of Commons, which we have just cause to believe to be an effect of the bloody counsels of Papists and other ill-affected persons, who have already raised a rebellion in the kingdom of Ireland; and by reason of many discoveries we cannot but fear they will proceed not only to stir up the like rebellion and insurrections in this kingdom of England, but also to back them with forces from abroad.

For the safety therefore of His Majesty's person, the Parliament and kingdom in this time of imminent danger:

It is ordained by the Lords and Commons now in Parliament assembled, that Henry Earl of Holland shall be Lieutenant of the County of Berks, Oliver Earl of Bolingbroke shall be Lieutenant of the County of Bedford, &c.

.   .   .   .

And shall severally and respectively have power to assemble and call together all and singular His Majesty's subjects, within the said several and respective counties and places, as well within liberties as without, that are meet and fit for the wars, and them to train and exercise and put in readiness, and from time to time to cause to be arrayed and weaponed, and to take the muster of them in places most fit for that purpose .   .   .   .

THE KING'S PROCLAMATION ON THE ORDINANCE, 27th MAY 1642

We do therefore, by this our Proclamation, expressly charge and command all our sheriffs, and all colonels, lieutenant-colonels, sergeant-majors, captains, officers and soldiers, belonging to the trained bands of this our kingdom, and likewise all high and petty constables, and other our officers and subjects whatsoever, upon their allegiance, and as they tender the peace of this our kingdom, not to muster, levy, raise or march, or to summon or warn, upon any warrant, order or ordinance from one or both of our Houses of Parliament (whereunto we have not, or shall not, give our express consent), any of our trained bands or other forces, to rise, muster,

march or exercise, without express warrant under our hand or
warrant from our sheriff of the county, grounded upon a particular
writ to that purpose under our Great Seal; and in case any of our
trained bands shall rise or gather together contrary to this our
command, we shall then call them in due time to a strict account,
and proceed legally against them, as violators of the laws and dis-
turbers of the peace of this kingdom.

Given at our Court of York

the 27th day of May 1642.

RESOLUTIONS OF THE HOUSES OF PARLIAMENT FOR RAISING AN ARMY, 12th JULY 1642

Resolved upon the question, that an army shall be forthwith
raised for the safety of the King's person, defence of both Houses
of Parliament, and of those who have obeyed their orders and
commands, and preserving of the true religion, the laws, liberty
and peace of the kingdom.

Resolved upon the question, that the Earl of Essex shall be
general.

Resolved upon the question, that this House doth declare, that
in this cause, for the safety of the King's person, defence of both
Houses of Parliament, and of those who have obeyed their orders
and commands, and preserving of the true religion, the laws, liberty
and peace of the kingdom, they will live and die with the Earl of
Essex, whom they have nominated general in this cause.

Resolved upon the question, that a petition shall be framed, to
move His Majesty to a good accord with his Parliament to prevent a
civil war.

CAVALIERS, LITERALLY

The advantage that King Charles I had: gentlemen then kept good horses, and many horses for a man-at-arms, and men that could ride them; hunting horses. Now we are come all to our coaches, forsooth!

JOHN AUBREY (1626–97), *Brief Lives*

FROM THE NORTH

Mrs. Eure, from Malton, Yorkshire, to Ralph Verney

5th May 1642 . . . I hope the Parliament will lay no more taxes on the country, for rents are paid nowhere.

7th May 1642 . . . O, that the sweet Parliament would come with the olive-branch in its mouth, it would refresh and glad all our hearts here in the North. We are so many frightened people; for my part if I hear but a door creak I take it to be a drum, and am ready to run out of that little valour I have.

21st May 1642 . . . the women in this county begin to rise; there hath been a hundred with the King, and above, to have their grievances redressed, and he hath given them so good content that they say he is as proper a man as is in England. I wish you all to take heed of women, for this very vermin have pulled down an enclosure which some of them were put in prison for by the justices, that had their pipe to go before them and their ale and cakes to make themselves merry when they had done their feats of activity. I write you this news to let you see what brave spirits is in the North. I wish all were well ended, for things stand in so ill a condition here as we can make no money of our coalpits. If rents fail and those fail too, we shall be in a hard case.

THE KING RAISES MONEY ABROAD TO PURCHASE ARMS

Order of the House of Commons, 2nd June 1642

. . . Whereas information has been given that the Jewels of the Crown (which by the law of the land ought not to be alienated) are either pawned or sold in Amsterdam, or some other part beyond the Seas, and thereby great sums of money . . . provided for His Majesty's use . . .

FROM LONDON

Thomas Barrow, from London, to Mrs. Katherine Oxinden, 7th June 1642

. . . News I cannot write any. I cannot see but that we are all in the way to be a miserable people, for here is nothing but distractions, the which makes me fear will bring us to confusion, and I pray God we may not have just cause to say that what we took to be our wealth be not unto us an occasion of falling; here is great, too great, fear of it, but we must submit to God's will, [may] he give us grace to take the true and right way and patience to bear whatever he sends . . .

FROM HERTFORDSHIRE

Lady Sussex to Ralph Verney

20th June 1642 . . . I am loth to eat in pewter yet, but truly I have put up most of my plate, and say 'tis sold, I hope they will send to borrow no money of my lord . . .

24th June 1642 . . . Both sides promise so fair that I cannot see what it is they should fight for. These fines and subsidies on both sides will be a ruin to this kingdom and us.

Petition of Gentlemen of Cornwall to the King, 26th June 1642

. . . we most humbly beseech your Majesty never to allow your subjects to be governed by an arbitrary government nor admit an alteration in Religion. And your Petitioners being most feelingly grieved for Your Majesty's discontents . . . do with a confluence of all comforts, honour and happiness unto Your Majesty, and do most heartily pray for the reconcilement between Your Majesty and your Parliament.

. . . your Petitioners do offer themselves most ready to maintain and defend, with their lives and fortunes, Your Majesty's sacred Person, Honour, Estate and lawful prerogative against all persons whatsoever, according to the oaths of supremacy and allegiance.

Lostwithiel, signed by John Gritts, High Sheriff and
7000 other Gentlemen

Men began to take sides — or some of them did; some, like the Earl of Kingston, tried to remain neutral, but in the end found it impossible. Men's motives were mixed, and on the side of Parliament were to be found such unpuritanical characters as Martin and Gell, for the War created strange bedfellows. Verney served the King, hopelessly, from loyalty, not from intellectual conviction. The Earl of Clare served himself, and he was not the only one to do so

Thomas Barrow, from London, to Henry Oxinden, 3rd July 1642

. . . Concerning news not in print, here is little. Here is great preparation for wars, but not against the King — happily not against his person — but Crown; yet we fight for Religion, but I declare our fight not for the true Protestant religion, that's the least of their thoughts, but for to maintain their new invented schismatical factions and their heretical opinions; and I do verily believe did you but see and know the passages I have seen and known, or had you but heard the discourses I heard from a Parliament man this day, you *would persist from being so strong a Parliamentarian*, and after

a short time I make no question but you will see some good cause
to alter your opinion; but, however, I hope though we differ in
opinion concerning King and Parliament, yet I hope we have one
Lord, one Faith, one Baptism, and if we have so, it is more than
many brothers now a day have, for here is now not only differences
between brothers but between fathers and children concerning faith
and baptism. I am afraid they will shortly find out a new God, but
enough of that subject . . .

[Amongst the King's supporters in Nottinghamshire, second
only to the Earl of Newcastle] was the Earl of Kingston, a man of
vast estate and no less covetous, who divided his sons between both
parties and concealed himself; till at length his fate drew him to
declare himself absolutely on the King's side, wherein he behaved
himself honourably and died remarkably.

.   .   .   .

The Earl of Kingston a few months stood neuter . . . They sent
Captain Lomax . . . to press him to declare for the Parliament, in so
needful a season. My lord, professing himself as rather desirous of
peace, and fully resolved not to act on either side, made a serious
imprecation of himself in these words: "When" said he "I take
arms with the King against the Parliament, or with the Parliament
against the King, let a cannon-bullet divide me between them;"
which God was pleased to bring to pass a few months after; for
he, going to Gainsborough, and there taking up arms for the King,
was surprised by my Lord Willoughby, and after a handsome
defence of himself, yielded, and was put prisoner into a pinnace,
and sent down the river to Hull; when my Lord Newcastle's army
marching along the shore, shot at the pinnace, and being in danger,
the Earl of Kingston went up on the deck to show himself and to
prevail with them to forbear shooting; but as soon as he appeared a
cannon-bullet flew from the King's army, and divided him in the

middle, and thus, being then in the Parliament's pinnace, he perished according to his own unhappy imprecation.

LUCY HUTCHINSON, *Memoirs of Colonel Hutchinson* (c. 1665: pubd. 1806)

Another account of the Earl's end.

. . . sent away the Earl of Kingston in a pinnace to Hull, which in its passage being espied by a party of the King's forces, they drew up some musketeers to the Trent-side and discharged at her, and unhappily killed the Earl and his man Savile in their cabin.

JOHN RUSHWORTH, *Historical Collections* (1659-1701)

His [Henry Martin's] father found out a rich wife for him, whom he married something unwillingly. He was a great lover of pretty girls, to whom he was so liberal that he spent the greatest part of his estate . . . He lived from his wife a long time. If I am not mistaken, she was sometime distempered by his unkindness to her.

King Charles I had complaint against him for his wenching. It happened that Henry was in Hyde Park one time when His Majesty was there, going to see a race. The King espied him and said aloud "Let that ugly rascal be gone out of the Park, that whoremaster, or else I will not see the sport." So Henry went away patiently. That sarcasm raised the whole county of Berks against [the King]: he [Martin] was as far from a Puritan as light from darkness. Shortly after (1641) he was chosen Knight of the Shire of that county, *nemine contradicente*, and proved a deadly enemy to the King.

. . . .

His speeches in the House were not long, but wondrous poignant, pertinent, and witty. He was exceeding happy in apt instances. He alone has sometimes turned the whole House. Making an invective speech one time against old Sir Henry Vane, when he had done with him he said, "But for young Sir Harry Vane — " and so sat him down. Several cried out, "What have you to say to young Sir Harry?" He rises up: "Why! if young Sir Harry lives to be old, he will be old Sir Harry!" and so sat down, and set the House alaughing, as he oftentimes did. Oliver Cromwell once in the House called him, jestingly or scoffingly, "*Sir* Harry Martin". H.M. rises and bows, "I thank *Your Majesty*, I always thought when you were *King* that I should be knighted." A godly member made a motion to have all profane and unsanctified persons expelled the Houses. H.M. stood up and moved that all fools might be put out likewise, and then there would be a thin House. He was wont to sleep much in the House (at least dog-sleep). Alderman Atkins made a motion that such scandalous members as slept and minded not the business of the House should be put out. H.M. starts up — "Mr. Speaker, a motion has been made to turn out the *Nodders*; I desire the *Noddees* may also be turned out."

JOHN AUBREY (1626–97), *Brief Lives*

No man knew for what reason he [Sir John Gell of Derbyshire] chose [the Parliament's] side: for he had not understanding enough to judge the equity of the cause, or piety or holiness; being a foul adulterer all the time he served the Parliament, and so unjust that without any remorse he suffered his men indifferently to plunder both honest men and cavaliers; so revengeful that he purused his malice to Sir John Stanhope . . . with such barbarism after his death that he, pretending to search for arms and plate, came into the church and defaced his monument that cost six hundred pounds, breaking off the nose and other parts of it. He dug up a garden of flowers, the only delight of his widow, upon the same pretence; and then wooed that widow . . . till, deluded by his hypocrisies, she was persuaded to marry him, and found that was the utmost point to which he could carry his revenge, his future carriage making it apparent he sought her for nothing else but to destroy the glory of her husband and his house.

LUCY HUTCHINSON, *Memoirs of Colonel Hutchinson*
(*c.* 1665; pubd. 1806)

Sir Edmund Verney in conversation with Edward Hyde (afterwards Lord Clarendon), August 1642

"I will willingly join with you the best I can, but I shall act it very scurvily. My condition is much worse than yours, and different I believe from any other man's, and will very well justify the melancholic that I confess to you possesses me. You have satisfaction in your conscience that you are in the right; that the King ought not to grant what is required of him; and so you do your duty and your business together. But for my part I do not like the quarrel, and do heartily wish that the King would yield and consent to what they desire; so that my conscience is only concerned in honour and gratitude to follow my master. I have eaten his bread and served him near thirty years, and will not do so base a thing as to forsake him: and choose rather to lose my life (which I am sure to do) to preserve and defend those things which are against my conscience to preserve and defend."

[Verney was killed two months later at Edgehill.]

CLARENDON, *History of the Rebellion* (1646–71: pubd. 1702–4)

The Earl of Clare was very often of both parties, and I think advantaged neither .... Sir Thomas Hutchinson continued with the Parliament, was firm to their cause, but infinitely desirous that the difference might rather have been composed by accommodation than ended by conquest; and therefore did not improve his interest to engage the country [*i.e.* county] in the quarrel, which, if he could have prevented, he would not have had come to a war.

LUCY HUTCHINSON, *Memoirs of Colonel Hutchinson*
(*c.* 1665; pubd. 1806)

c

THE FIRST CIVIL WAR

As for the soldiers on either side, the fearful civilians found there was not much to choose between them.

Sir Thomas Peyton, from London, to Henry Oxinden,
14th May 1640

. . . The troopers do commit many outrages in their passage, as firing of towns, ravishing of women (which others of the sex would perhaps call courtesy of soldiers, as it is the end of all compliment and observances at Court), stealing or violent taking; which is a presage of much future disorder. Death's harbinger, the sword, famine and other plagues that hang over us are ready to swallow up the wicked Age . . .

House of Commons, 12th March 1641

A complaint that the Northern Army was in disorder for want of discipline by martial law; yet the Commons being tender to yield thereunto no order was made.

. . . Colonel Robert Gibbons in charge of the Parliamentarian forces . . . came into the church of Goudhurst, Mr. Willcocks in his sermon, and called unto him (having soldiers to second his doings), "Sirrah, you that stand prating there, come down, or I will shoot you down", and so carried him prisoner up to London.
Note-book of Sir Roger Twysden (1597–1672)

Sir Thomas Gardiner, from Cuddesdon, to Ralph Verney, September 1642

. . . One extravagant word, spoken but by one man, is enough to confiscate the goods of a whole family to the Parliament soldiers . . . The gentry (say they) have been our masters a long time and now we may chance to master them, and now they know their strength it shall go hard but they will use it . . .

Memorandum by Sir Robert Filmer, of East Sutton, Kent

Upon the first of September 1642, Sir Robert Filmer had his horse, arms, furniture [*i.e.* horse's equipment], pistols, muskets, powder, bullets and many other things taken away by troopers of Captain Sandys' [of the Parliament's army] and his bedding then burnt by them, and his house being in great danger of being fired by them, he being neither delinquent nor having refused to give or lend to the Parliament.

Lady Gardiner, from Cuddesdon, to her brother, Ralph Verney, 30th September 1642

. . . i am in a grt dill of vexsation for pore Oxford, for this day ther is 12 hondored solgars come ther, and I am afrad that they will make a grit masacar of all the books. They du threten them ex-stremly . . .

Thomas Hilder and Thomas Wheller, from London, to the Mayor and Corporation of Sandwich, 17th November 1642

. . . The Cavaliers are extremely outrageous in plundering where they come, putting no difference at all between friends, and supposed enemies in that kind . . . These malignants, when they have enjoyed in inns all accommodations that could possibly be afforded, then they have at their parting taken all that hath been useful for them away and ripped up feather-beds and thrown the feathers in the wind to be blown away for sport, and scanned all the barrels of beer and wine and spilt it in their cellars. They have killed of one man's 1000 sheep and thrown away such of it as they could not eat, many other outrages they commit too large to express this way. . .

Thomas Denne, from London, to Henry Oxinden,
15th November 1642

Sir, The news here is so contrary and the times so troublesome that he is quietest that writes none. The shops here have been shut up above these ten days, and all those that the Parliament cannot confide in they take away their arms and secure their persons; there is at least 800 in this City on the Roll for Malignants, being some Aldermen, some merchants, etc. [The] City is well fortified against the [Cav]aliers and had so many ordnance [that it] is almost invulnerable.

PROCLAMATION BY THE KING
25th NOVEMBER 1642

We have taken into Our Princely and serious consideration the great misery and ruin falling and like to fall upon Our good subjects (if not timely prevented) by the plundering, robbing and spoiling of their houses, and taking from them their money, plate, household stuff, cattle and other goods . . . and these unjust and unlawful actions done by divers soldiers of Our Army and others sheltering themselves in the same, under that title . . . declare Our Royal pleasure to be that from henceforth no officer, soldier of horse or foot or party sent from Our Army presume to search for or seize upon any money, plate, goods or household stuff, without Our express warrant for the same under Our sign manual . . .

[c. December 1642] Although the town [Nottingham] was generally more malignant than well-affected [i.e. Royalist rather than Parliamentarian] yet they cared not much to have cavalier soldiers quarter with them, and therefore agreed to defend themselves against any force which should come against them.

LUCY HUTCHINSON, *Memoirs of Colonel Hutchinson*
(c. 1665; pubd. 1806)

Henry Oxinden to Katherine Barrow [Spring, 1643]

Dearest Sister, I received your letter wherein you certify me of the danger of plundering; if you will follow my advice, rather give a little than lose all. Whoever shall hap to be undone by the plunderers at either side, it is a thousand to one if ever they be made whole either by King or Parliament . . .

Lady Sussex, from Gorhambury, Herts., to Sir Ralph Verney, November 1643

. . . My fear is most of Prince Rupert, for they say he has little mercy when he comes . . . I have made up some of the doors and piled them so with wood that I believe my house is able to keep out a good many now; if we escape plundering I shall account it a great mercy of God; they are all about us here in such grievous fears that if they see but a gentleman riding they think it is to rob them.

But not all the soldiers were so war-like.

Dorset, 1642

. . . the Parliament's soldiers of the Militia not enduring to lie long in the field, it being harvest-time, left the Commissioners and went home to their own houses to mind their Harvest.

JOHN RUSHWORTH, *Historical Collections* (1659–1701)

Prince Rupert, aged 23, became the Royalist commander of horse. Pepys' brief comment, eighteen years later, seems to sum up the general attitude towards him.

Order to Sir John Heydon, Lieutenant General of the King's ordnance at Oxford

These are to will and require you forthwith upon sight and receipt hereof to deliver to this bearer for the arming of mine own troop in His Majesty's present service, 30 pair of your best holster and as many of your best spanners and as many of your best flasks as also one hundred weight of pistol shot (and 100 weight of carbine shot) of the most ordinary bore or gauge (also 6 powder bags for Prince Maurice his regiment) hereof you must not fail . . . Given at Packington Heath the 19th October 1642.

Rupert

. . . the old General was set aside and Prince Rupert put into the command, which was no popular change, for the other was known to be an officer of great experience and had committed no oversights in his conduct, was willing to hear everything debated and always concurred with the most reasonable opinion . . . The Prince was rough and passionate, and loved not debate, liked what was proposed as he liked the person who proposed it, and was so great an

enemy to Digby and Culpepper, who were only present in debates
of the War with the officers, that he crossed all they proposed.

CLARENDON, *History of the Rebellion* (1646–71;
pubd. 1702–4)

29th September 1660. This day or yesterday, I hear, Prince Rupert
is come to Court; but welcome to nobody.

Pepys' Diary

THE BATTLE OF EDGEHILL, 23rd OCTOBER 1642

Sir Jacob Astley's prayer before the battle:

> O Lord, thou knowest how busy I must be this day. If I forget
> Thee, do not Thou forget me. March on, boys!

A relation of the Battle printed by His Majesty's command:

> . . . If we had had light enough to have given one charge more
> we had totally routed all their army, whereupon both armies
> retreated, ours in such order that we not only brought off our own
> cannon but four of the rebels' . . . For the slain on both sides the
> number is uncertain; yet it is most certain that we have killed
> five for one . . .

A relation of the Battle communicated to the Speaker and Commons:

> . . . a blessed victory which God hath given us upon the army
> of cavaliers and of those evil persons who upon Sunday 23 of this
> instant engaged His Majesty in a dangerous and bloody fight
> against his faithful subjects . . .

Lady Sussex to Sir Ralph Verney, 14th January, 1643

> . . . Sometimes when there is any true things put in print, I
> should be glad of them; but not of all the idle things they make.

THE GHOSTS OF EDGEHILL

Portentious apparitions of two jarring and contrary armies where the battle was strucken were seen at Edge Hill, where are still many unburied carcases, at between Twelve and one of the clock in the morning. As was certified by Persons of Quality. These infernal soldiers appeared on Christmas night, and again on two Saturdays after, bearing the King's and Parliament's colours. Pell nell to it they went, where the corporeal armies had shed so much blood, the clattering of arms, noise of cannons, cries of soldiers, sounds of petronels, and the alarum was struck up, creating great terror and amazement. The rumour whereof coming to His Majesty at Oxford, he sent Colonel Kirke and five other gentlemen of Credit, who all saw the forementioned prodigies, distinctly knowing divers of the apparitions and incorporeal substances by their faces . . .

Pamphlet published in January 1643

In 1642/3, after Edgehill fight, his Sir John Denham's poem called *Cowper's Hill* was printed at Oxford, in a sort of brown paper, for then they could get no better.

JOHN AUBREY (1626–97), *Brief Lives*

A lucky accident at the attack on Tadcaster, November 1642

And here again there fell out another remarkable Providence. During this conflict, our magazine was blown up: which struck such a terror in the enemy, thinking we had cannon (which they were informed we had not) that they instantly retreated. And though I had but a few horse, they pursued the enemy some miles, and took many prisoners.

Fairfax's Memorials (? 1665)

THE TAKING OF MARLBOROUGH, WILTSHIRE, BY THE ROYALISTS, 5th DECEMBER 1642

. . . Having thus won the town they set fire to it in two other places so that there were four fires blazing at once, and the soldiers fell to pillaging the houses and shops, all the wearing apparel, plate and money they took away and all the horses and carts that were in the town . . . On the Tuesday they carried away the prisoners being in number between 100 and 120, marching on foot, tied two and two together, before the cannon to Oxford . . . There were 53 houses burnt and the damage sustained by the town (besides the value of these houses) in goods, money and ware, was computed to amount to near 50,000 £.

JOHN RUSHWORTH, *Historical Collections* (1659–1701)

In some places the gentlemen on both sides sought to withdraw their county from the War, as did these of Cheshire. But Parliament declared against this agreement for neutrality.

30 December 1642. Agreement made at Bunbury in the county of Chester for a pacification and settling of the peace of that county.

1. It is agreed that there be an absolute cessation of arms from henceforth within this county and no arms taken up to offend one another, but by the consent of the King and both Houses of Parliament, unless it be to resist forces brought into the county . . .

2. That all but 200 of either side shall be disbanded tomorrow, being Saturday, and on Monday all the rest, on both sides, both Horse and Foot, shall be disbanded.

3. That all prisoners on both sides shall be enlarged.

5. That all goods and arms taken on both sides now remaining in the county in specie be forthwith restored . . .

.   .   .   .

8. Lastly, all the said parties do agree and promise to each other, on the word of a gentleman, as they desire to prosper, that as well themselves as also all their friends, tenants, servants and all others in whom they have an interest shall, as much as in them lies, perform the agreement . . .

FIRE-WATCHERS IN HULL, SPRING 1643

My Lord of Newcastle now lay siege to Hull . . . upon a bank, which was the highway, he approached so near as to shoot cannon shot at random into the town; which were for the most part fiery bullets. But the diligence and care of the Governor (who caused every inhabitant to watch his own house, and wheresoever they saw these bullets fall, to be ready to quench them) prevented the danger.

Fairfax's Memorials (? 1665)

DEATH OF HAMPDEN

Prince Rupert with a strong party frequently beat up the Parliament quarters as at Postcombe and Chinnor in Oxfordshire: and sometimes made incursions into Buckinghamshire, whose forces were drawn together in Chalgrove Field to resist him: but on the 18th June, 1643 the Prince engaged them and put them to the rout . . . Mr. Hampden (one of the five members) who would go out with this party contrary to the advice of his friends, being not ordered to it, was wounded and died thereof, June 24th, his death being much lamented by the Parliament party.

JOHN RUSHWORTH, *Historical Collections* (1659–1701)

Between the gentlemen on both sides courtesies were still practised.

During that war 'twas his [Sir William Davenant's] hap to have two aldermen of York his prisoners, who were something stubborn and would not give the ransom ordered by the Council of War. Sir William used them civilly, and treated them in his tent, and sat them at the upper end of his table *à la mode de France*, and having done so a good while to his charge told them (privately and friendly) that he was not able to keep so chargeable guests, and bade them take an opportunity to escape, which they did; but having been gone a little way they considered with themselves that in gratitude they ought to go back and give Sir William their thanks; which they did, but it was like to have been to their great danger of being taken by the soldiers; but they happened to get safe to York.

The King's party being overcome, Sir William Davenant . . . went into France.

. . . .

Sir William was brought prisoner to England. Whether he was first a prisoner at Carisbrooke Castle in the Isle of Wight, or at the Tower of London, I have forgot; he was a prisoner at both . . . He expected no mercy from the Parliament, and had no hopes of escaping his life. It pleased God that the two aldermen of York aforesaid hearing that he was taken and brought to London to be tried for his life, which they understood was in extreme danger, they were touched with so much generosity and goodness, as, upon their own accounts and mere motion, to try what they could to save Sir William's life who had been so civil to them and a means to save theirs, upon their petition, etc., Sir William's life was saved. ('Twas Harry Martin that saved Sir William Davenant's life in the House. When they were talking of sacrificing one, then said Henry that "in sacrifices they always offered pure and without blemish: now ye talk of making a sacrifice of an old rotten rascal." *Vide* H. Martin's Life, where *by this very jest*, then forgot, the Lord Falkland saved H. Martin's life. [in 1660])

JOHN AUBREY (1626–97) *Brief Lives*

And not many days after [July 1643] the Earl of Newcastle sent my wife back again, in his coach, with some horse to guard her: which generosity gained more than any reputation he could have gotten in detaining a lady prisoner upon such terms.

Fairfax's Memorials (? 1665)

He [Newcastle] liked the pomp and absolute authority of a General well and preserved the dignity of it to the full; and for the discharge of the outward state and circumstances of it, in acts of courtesy, affability, bounty and generosity, he abounded; which, in the infancy of a war, made him, for some time, very acceptable to men of all conditions. But the substantial part, and fatigue of a General, he did not in any degree understand (being utterly unacquainted with war) nor could submit to . . . In all actions of the field he was still present and never absent in any battle; in all which he gave instances of an invincible courage and fearlessness in danger . . . Such articles of action were no sooner over than he retired to his delightful company, music, or his softer pleasures, to all which he was so indulgent and to his ease that he would not be interrupted upon what occasion soever, insomuch as he sometimes denied admission to the chiefest officers of the army . . . for two days together; from whence many inconveniences fell out.

CLARENDON, *History of the Rebellion* (1646–71;
pubd. 1702–4)

The next two extracts give some idea of the personal bravery and essential decency of Fairfax, the Parliamentarian General of Horse.

Here [at the fight at Selby, 2nd July 1643] I received a shot in the wrist of my arm, which made the bridle fall out of my hand; which, being among the nerves and veins, suddenly let out such a quantity of blood as that I was ready to fall from my horse. So taking the reins in the other hand, wherein I had my sword, the enemy minding nothing so much as how to get away, I drew myself out of the crowd, and came to our men . . . Seeing me ready to fall from my horse they laid me on the ground, now almost senseless. My Chirurgeon came seasonable and bound up the wound, so stopped the bleeding.

After a quarter of an hour's rest there I got on horseback again.

Fairfax's Memorials (? 1665)

And here I cannot omit a remarkable passage of Divine Justice. Whilst we were engaged in the fight with those horse that entered the gate [at Adwalton Moor, 30th June 1643] four soldiers had stripped Colonel Herne naked as he lay dead upon the ground, men still fighting round about him: and so dexterous were these villains as they had done it and mounted themselves again before we had beaten them off. But after we had beaten them to their ordnance . . . and returning to our ground again, the enemy discharged a piece of cannon in our rear. The bullet fell into Captain Copley's troop, in which those four men were: two of whom were killed and some hurt or mark remained on the rest, though dispersed into several ranks of the troop, which was [the] more remarkable.

We had not yet Martial Law amongst us: which gave me a good occasion to reprove it, by showing the soldiers the sinfulness of the act, and how GOD would punish when men wanted power to do it.

Fairfax's Memorials (? 1665)

Like Dr. Plumptre, some men remained more concerned about their private possessions than the common weal.

. . . Dr. Plumptre (a horrible atheist, and had such an intolerable pride, that he brooked no superiors), hearing that the [Parliamentarian] forces were to march away, was raging at it; whereupon, being answered that it was more for the public interest of the cause in great passion he replied, "What is the cause to me, if my goods be lost?"

LUCY HUTCHINSON, *Memoirs of Colonel Hutchinson*
(*c.* 1665; pubd. 1806)

Cromwell sent the following letter to the newspapers following his victory at Grantham the same day.

Grantham, 13th May 1643

Sir,

God hath given us, this evening, a glorious victory over our enemies. They were, as we are informed one-and-twenty colours of horse troops, and three or four of dragoons.

It was late in the evening when we drew out; they came and faced us within two miles of the town. So soon as we had the alarm, we drew out our forces, consisting of about twelve troops, whereof some of them so poor and broken that you shall seldom see worse: with this handful it pleased God to cast the scale. For after we had stood a little, above musket-shot the one body from the other, and the dragooners had fired on both sides for the space of half an hour or more; they not advancing towards us we agreed to charge them. And advancing the body after many shots on both sides, we came on with our troops a pretty round trot, they standing firm to receive us: and our men charging fiercely upon them, by God's providence they were completely routed, and ran all away, and we had the execution of them two or three miles.

I believe some of our soldiers did kill two or three men apiece in the pursuit; but what the number of dead is we are not certain. We took forty-five Prisoners, besides diverse of their horse and arms, and rescued many Prisoners whom they had lately taken of ours; and we took four or five of their colours.

Oliver Cromwell

But the printed news was unreliable, rumours abounded, and it was difficult to find out what was happening.

Thomas Barrow, from London, to Henry Oxinden [May 1643]

. . . For news, I doubt not but you have had a confident report of the taking of Reading and Oxford, both which I desire you believe alike, for both are very contrary to truth . . . I also hear that this day an act of Common Council passed that the Cross in Cheapside should be pulled down; if that takes now, then Paul's is soon after to follow, and so other churches by degrees; the windows in St. Margaret's, Westminster were battered to pieces on Tuesday last . . .

Throughout the summer Cromwell sent reports, and urgent requests for help, to the Eastern Counties Association.

Oliver Cromwell, to the Corporation of Colchester, 28th May 1643

I thought it my duty to write once more unto you for more strength to be speedily sent unto us for this great service.

I suppose you hear of the great defeat given by my Lord Fairfax to the Newcastle forces at Wakefield. It was a great mercy of God to us. And had it not been bestowed upon us at this very present, my Lord Fairfax had not known how to have subsisted. We assure you, should the force we have miscarry, expect nothing but a speedy march of the Enemy up unto you.

Why you should not strengthen us to make us subsist, judge you the danger of the neglect; and how inconvenient this improvidence, or unthrift, may be to you . . . The Enemy draws more to the Lord Fairfax: our motion and yours must be exceeding speedy, or else it will do you no good at all.

If you send, let your men come to Boston. I beseech you hasten the supply to us. Forget not money: I press not hard, though I do so need that, I assure you, the foot and dragooners are ready to mutiny. Lay not too much upon the back of a poor gentleman who desires, without much noise, to lay down his life and bleed the last drop to serve the Cause and you. I ask not your money for myself; if that were my end and hope, *viz.* the pay of my place, I would not open my mouth at this time. I desire to deny myself, but others will not be satisfied. I beseech you hasten supplies. Forget not your prayers.

Oliver Cromwell, from Huntingdon, to Sir Edmund Bacon, Sir William Spring, Sir Thomas Barnardiston, and Maurice Barrow, [of the Eastern Counties Association Committee,] 31st July 1643

[Cromwell's force, with 300 Nottinghamshire men and men from Lincoln, advance towards Gainsborough.]

. . . About a mile and a half from the town we met a forlorn hope of the enemy of near 100 horse. Our dragooners laboured to beat them back; but not alighting off their horses the enemy charged them, and beat some four or five off their horses: our horse charged them, and made them retire unto their main body. We advanced and came to the bottom of a steep hill. We could not well get up but by some tracks, which our men essaying to do, a body of the enemy endeavoured to hinder, wherein we prevailed and got to the top of the hill. This was done by the Lincolners, who had the vanguard.

When we all recovered the top of the hill, we saw a great body of the enemy's horse facing us, at about a musket-shot or less distance, and a good reserve of a full Regiment of horse behind it. We endeavoured to put our men into as good order as we could. The enemy in the meantime advanced towards us, to take us at disadvantage; but in such order as we were we charged their great body, I having the right wing. We came up horse to horse, where we disputed it with our swords and pistols a pretty time, all keeping close order so that one could not break the other. At last they a little shrinking, our men perceiving it, pressed in upon them and immediately routed this whole body; some flying on one side and others on the other of the enemy's reserve; and our men pursuing them had chase and execution about five or six miles.

. . . We then, after this defeat which was so total, relieved the town with such powder and provision as we brought. Which done, we had notice that there were six troops of horse and 300 foot on the other side of the town, about a mile off us; we desired some foot of my Lord Willoughby's, about 400, and with our horse and these foot marched towards them. When we came towards the place at which their horse stood, we beat back with my troops about two or three troops of the enemy's, who retired into a small village at the bottom of the hill. When we recovered the hill we saw in the bottom, about quarter of a mile from us, a regiment of foot; after that, another; after that the Marquis of Newcastle's own Regiment: consisting in all of about 50 foot colours, and a great body of horse — which indeed was Newcastle's Army. Which, coming so unexpectedly, put us to new consultations. My Lord Willoughby and I, being in the town, agreed to call off our foot. I went to bring them off; but before I returned divers of the foot were engaged, the enemy advancing with his whole body. Our foot retreated in disorder and with some loss got the town, where they now are. Our horse also came off with some trouble, being wearied with the long fight and their horses tired, yet faced the enemy's fresh horse and by several removes got off without the loss of one man, the enemy following the rear with a great body.

The honour of this retreat is due to God, as also all the rest . . .

What you are to do upon it is next to be considered. . . . If you will raise 2000 foot at present to encounter this Army of Newcastle's, to raise the siege and to enable us to fight him, we doubt not, by the grace of God, but that we shall be able to relieve the town and beat the enemy [to] the other side of the Trent. Whereas if somewhat be not done in this, you will see Newcastle's Army march up into your bowels, being now, as it is, on this side Trent. I know that it will be difficult to raise thus many in so short time, but let me assure you, it's necessary, and therefore to be done. At least, do what you may, with all possible expedition. I would I had the happiness to speak with one of you: truly I cannot come over, but must attend my charge, the Enemy is vigilant. The Lord direct you what to do.

Oliver Cromwell, from Huntingdon, to the Commissioners at Cambridge, 6th August 1643

You see by this enclosed how sadly your affairs stand. It's no longer Disputing, but Out instantly all you can. Raise all your Bands, send them to Huntingdon: get up what volunteers you can: hasten your Horses.

Send these letters to Norfolk, Suffolk, and Essex without delay. I beseech you spare not, but be expeditious and industrious. Almost all our Foot have quitted Stamford; there is nothing to interrupt an Enemy but our Horse that is considerable. You must act lively: do it without distraction. Neglect no means.

Oliver Cromwell, from Peterborough, to the Commissioners at Cambridge, 8th August 1643

. . . The money I brought with me is so poor a pittance when it comes to be distributed amongst all my troops that, considering their necessity, it will not half clothe them, they were so far behind; if we have not more money immediately they will be exceedingly discouraged. I am sorry you put me to it to write thus often. It makes it seem a needless importunity in me, whereas in truth it is a constant neglect of those that should provide for us. Gentlemen, make them able to live and subsist that are willing to spend their blood for you — I say no more, but rest your faithful servant.

Oliver Cromwell to the Commissioners at Cambridge,
September 1643

I have been now two days in Cambridge, in expectation to hear
the fruit of your endeavours in Suffolk towards the public assistance. Believe it, you will hear of a storm in few days. You have
no Infantry at all considerable; hasten your Horses — a few hours
may undo you, neglected. I beseech you, be careful what Captains
of Horse you choose, what men be mounted: a few honest men
are better than numbers . . . If you choose honest Godly men to
be Captains of Horse, honest men will follow them; and they will
be careful to mount such . . . I had rather have a plain russet-coated
Captain that knows what he fights for and loves what he knows,
than that which you call "a Gentleman" and is nothing else. I
honour a Gentleman that is so indeed . . .

Oliver Cromwell to Oliver St. John, 11th September 1643

. . . I desire not to seek myself — I have little money of my own
to help my soldiers. My estate is little. I tell you the business of
Ireland and England hath had of me, in money, between Eleven
and Twelve Hundred pounds: therefore my Private can do little
to help the Public. You have had my money: I hope in God I
desire to venture my skin. So do mine. Lay weight upon their
patience, but break it not. Think of that which may be a real
help. I believe [?] 5,000 l. is due.

If you lay aside the thought of me and my letter I expect no
help.

*At the first Battle of Newbury, 20th September 1643, Lucius Cary,
Viscount Falkland, was killed. Did he throw away his life in despair of
the King's cause, or in remorse for the death of his mistress?*

. . . In this unhappy battle was slain the Lord Viscount Falkland, a
person of such prodigious parts of learning and knowledge, of that
inimitable sweetness and delight in conversation, of so flowing and
obliging a humanity and goodness to mankind, and of that primi-
tive simplicity and integrity of life, that if there were no other brand
upon this odious and accursed Civil War than that single loss,
it must be most infamous and execrable to all posterity . . . He was
so great an enemy to that passion and uncharitableness which he
saw produced by difference of opinion in matters of religion that
in all those disputations with priests and others of the Roman
Church, he affected to manifest all possible civility to their persons
and estimation of their parts . . . He was superior to all those passions
and affections which attend vulgar minds, and was guilty of no other
ambition than knowledge and to be reputed a lover of all good men
. . . He submitted to the King's command and became his Secretary . . . yet two things he could never bring himself to whilst he
continued in that office (that was, to his death) for which he was
contented to be reproached . . . the one, employment of spies . . .
the other, the liberty of opening letters . . .

He had a courage of the most clear and keen temper and in all
such encounters he had about him a strange cheerfulness and com-
panionableness, without at all affecting the execution that was then
principally to be attended, in which he took no delight, but took
pains to prevent it where it was not by resistance necessary, insomuch that at Edgehill, when the enemy was routed, he was like to
have incurred great peril by interposing to save those who had
thrown away their arms . . .

[In the House of Commons] when there was any overture or
hope of peace, he would be more erect and vigorous and exceedingly
solicitous to press anything which he thought might promote it,
and sitting amongst his friends often after a deep silence and frequent
sighs, would with a shrill and sad accent ingeminate the word

"Peace, peace", and would passionately profess that the very agony of the War, and the view of the calamities and desolation the Kingdom did and must endure, took his sleep from him, and would shortly break his heart . . .

In the morning before the battle, as always upon action, he was very cheerful and put himself into the first rank of the Lord Byron's Regiment, who was then advancing upon the enemy, who had lined the hedges on both sides with musketeers, from whence he was shot with a musket on the lower part of the belly, and in the instant falling from his horse, his body was not found until the next morning.

CLARENDON, *History of the Rebellion* (1646–71; pubd. 1702–4)

The Lord Viscount Falkland, His Majesty's Principal Secretary of State, who in the morning of the battle called for a clean shirt, saying That if he were slain they should not find his body in foul linen. Some of his friends dissuaded him from venturing himself as having no call to it, being no military officer; but he replied, That he was weary of the times and foresaw much misery to his own country, and did believe he should be out of it by night.

JOHN RUSHWORTH, *Historical Collections* (1659–1701)

In the Civil Wars he [Viscount Falkland] adhered to King Charles I, who after Edgehill fight made him Principal Secretary of Estate (with Sir Edward Nicholas), which he discharged with a great deal of wit and prudence, only his advice was very unlucky to His Majesty, in persuading him (after the victory at Roundway Down and the taking of Bristol) to sit down before Gloucester, which was so bravely defended by that incomparably vigilant Governor Colonel Massey and the diligent and careful soldiers and citizens (men and women), so that it so broke and weakened the King's

army that 'twas the procatractic cause of his ruin. After this all the
King's matters went worse and worse. *Anno domini* 1643 at the fight
at Newbury, my Lord Falkland being there, and having nothing
to do to charge; as the two armies were engaging rode in like
a mad-man (as he was) between them, and was (as he needs must
be) shot. Some, that were your superfine discoursing politicians
and fine gentlemen, would needs have the reason of this mad
action of throwing away his life so, to be his discontent for the
unfortunate advice given to his master as aforesaid; but, I have
been well informed by those that best knew him, and knew the
intrigues behind the curtain (as they say), that it was the grief of
the death of Mistress Moray, a handsome lady at Court, who was
his mistress, and whom he loved above all creatures, was the true
cause of his being so madly guilty of his own death, as aforementioned: (*nullum magnum ingenium sine mixtura dementiae*).

JOHN AUBREY (1626–97), *Brief Lives*

*Many of the common sort were also slain and injured. This account
of George Robinson's plight can stand for hundreds of others. Eight years
after the battle he was awarded a grant of 10s. in hand and an annual
pension of 40s.*

To the Right Worshipful the Judge and Justices assembled at the
General Quarter Session holden at the Old Castle of Canterbury,
the 22th July, 1651

The most humble petition of George Robinson, of the said
city, heelmaker.

Your worships' said poor petitioner going in the Parliament's
service under the command of Colonel Springet and in the company
whereof Mr William Jones was Captain, at the first fight at Newbury
was shot in one of his legs by means whereof he lay in the Hospital
of Bartholomew near Smithfield in London by the space of half a

year, lame and sore diseased in his body. And another half year after his departure thence in a chirurgeon's hand before he was able to work, having had above three-score splinters of the bone of his leg at several times taken out, to his great pains, and his own and his friends' great charge, whereby he is not alone disabled to follow his vocation but is almost continually in intolerable pain thereof, of which he cannot hope of remedy during his life.

In compassion whereof he most humbly beseecheth your good worships to bestow on him such pension towards his relief as to your wisdoms shall seem meet.

In doing whereof you shall bind him and his ever to pray for your worships' perpetual happiness.

Money, the sinews of war, was never sufficiently plentiful. This is an early example of a long series of requests by Cromwell for support, financial or in men.

To all and every the Inhabitants of Fen Drayton in the Hundred of Papworth [Cambridgeshire].

Whereas we have been enforced, by apparent grounds of approaching danger, to begin to fortify the Town of Cambridge, for preventing the Enemy's inroad, and the better to maintain the peace of this County:

Having in part seen your good affections to the Cause, and now standing in need of your further assistance to the perfecting of the said Fortifications, which will cost at least Two Thousand Pounds. We are encouraged as well as necessitated to desire a Freewill Offering of a Liberal Contribution from you, for the better enabling of us to attain our desired ends, *viz.*, the Preservation of our County, knowing that every honest and well affected man, considering the vast expenses we have already been at and our willingness to do

according to our ability, will be ready to contribute his best assistance to a work of so high concernment and so good an end.

We do therefore desire that what shall be by you freely given
and collected may with all convenient speed be sent to the Commissioners at Cambridge, to be employed to the use aforesaid.
And so you shall engage us to be

Yours ready to serve,

Oliver Cromwell
Thomas Martyn (and others)

Cambridge, this 8th of March, 1643.

The doubtful practice of humanity to the enemies of God.

[Autumn 1643] After our wounded men were dressed, as she
[Mrs. Hutchinson] stood at her chamber-door, seeing three of the
prisoners sorely cut and carried down bleeding into the Lion's
Den [*i.e.* the dungeon at Nottingham Castle], she desired the marshal
to bring them into her, and bound up and dressed their wounds
also: which while she was doing Captain Palmer came in and told
her his soul abhorred to see this favour to the enemies of God; she
replied, she had done nothing but what she thought was her duty
in humanity to them as fellow-creatures, not as enemies. But he
was very ill satisfied with her, and with the Governor (Colonel
Hutchinson) presently after, when he came into a very large room
where a very great supper was prepared, and more room and meat
than guests; to fill up which the Governor had sent for one, Mr.
Mason, one of the prisoners, a man of good fashion who had
married a relation of his, and was brought up more in fury than for
any proof of guilt in him, and I know not whether two or three
others the Governor had not called to meat with him; for which
Captain Palmer bellowed loudly against him, as a favourer of
malignants and cavaliers.

LUCY HUTCHINSON, *Memoirs of Colonel Hutchinson*
(*c.* 1665; pubd. 1806)

The choice of officers and men.

Oliver Cromwell to the Commissioners at Cambridge,
28th September 1643

. . . It may be it provokes some spirits to see such plain men made
Captains of Horse. It had been well that men of honour and birth
had entered into these employments: but why do they not appear?
Who would have hindered them? But seeing it was necessary the
work must go on, better plain men than none; but best to have
men patient of wants, faithfull and conscientious in their employment. And such, I hope, these will approve themselves to be . . .

Oliver Cromwell, from Cambridge, to Major-General Crawford,
10th March 1644

. . . Sir, the State, in choosing men to serve it, takes no notice of
their opinions; if they be willing faithfully to serve it, that satisfies.

*The first sentence of this account of the fight at Winceby on the 11th
October 1643 illustrates one of the continuing difficulties of the commanders
on both sides, namely the lack of intelligence.*

. . . I believe that as we had no notice of the enemy's coming
towards us, so they had as little of our preparation to fight with
them. It was about twelve of the clock ere our horse and dragooners
were drawn up. After that we marched about a mile nearer the
enemy; and then we began to descry him, by little and little, coming
towards us. Until this time we did not know we should fight; but
so soon as our men had knowledge of the enemy's coming they
were very full of joy and resolution, thinking it a great mercy that
they should now fight with him. Our men went on in several
bodies, singing Psalms . . .

Both they and we had drawn up our dragooners; who gave the first charge; and then the horse fell in. Colonel Cromwell fell with brave resolution upon the enemy, immediately after their dragooners had given him the first volley; yet they were so nimble as that, within half pistol shot, they gave him another: his horse was killed under him at the first charge, and fell down upon him; and as he rose up he was knocked down again by the Gentleman who charged him . . . but afterwards he recovered a poor horse in a soldier's hands, and bravely mounted himself again. Truly this first charge was so home-given and performed with so much admirable courage and resolution by our troops, that the enemy stood not another; but were driven back upon their own body which was to have seconded them; and at last put these into a plain disorder; and thus in less than half an hour's fight they were all quite routed . . . Above a hundred of their men were found drowned in ditches . . .

JOHN VICARS, *God's Ark overtopping the World's Waves, or the Third Part of the Parliamentary Chronicle* (1644)

The Royalist commander confesses to his defeat in a letter intercepted by the Parliamentarian forces.

Sir William Widdrington to the Marquis of Newcastle, 12th October 1643

. . . Saville's regiment totally running away, disordered and so put to rout our whole army. We have in a manner totally lost our foot and dragoons that were there, being near 800 horse extremely dispersed, but no great number cut off.

The danger of letter-writing.

Sir Thomas Peyton, from London, to Henry Oxinden,
20th October 1643

. . . But I have writ too much, I am afraid, especially if my
letter be intercepted, which is not ashamed, however, of any light . . .

*The ebb and flow of courage and cowardice on both sides in a Royalist
attack on Nottingham, January 1644.*

. . . Many of the attackers ran away and many of their horses were
quite spoiled: for two miles they left a great track of blood, which
froze as it fell upon the snow, for it was such bitter weather that the
foot had waded almost to the middle in snow as they came, and
were so numbed with cold when they came into the town that they
were fain to be rubbed to get life into them, and in that condition
were more eager for fires and warm meat than for plunder . . .
Indeed, no one can believe but those that saw that day, what a
strange ebb and flow of courage and of cowardice there was in both
parties on that day. The cavaliers marched in with such terror to
the garrison and such gallantry that they startled not when one of
their leading files fell before them all at once, but marched boldly
over the dead bodies of their friends, under their enemies' cannon,
and carried such valiant dreadfulness about them as made very
courageous stout men recoil. Our horse, who ran away frightened
at the sight of their foes, when they had breastworks before them
and the advantage of freshness to beat back assailants already
vanquished with the sharpness of the cold and a killing march,
within three or four hours, as men that thought nothing too great
for them, returned fiercely upon the same men, after their refresh-
ment, when they were entered into defensible houses. If it were a
romance, one should say, after the success, that the heroes did it

out of excess of gallantry that they might the better signalise their valour upon a foe who was not vanquished to their hands by the inclemency of the season: but we are relating wonders of Providence and must record this as one not to be conceived of, but by those who saw and shared in it.

LUCY HUTCHINSON, *Memoirs of Colonel Hutchinson*
(c. 1665; pubd. 1806)

"If my soldiers get out of hand it will be your fault."

Oliver Cromwell, at Ely, to the Rev. Mr. Hitch, 10th January 1644

Mr. Hitch,

Lest the soldiers should in any tumultuary or disorderly way attempt the Reformation of the Cathedral Church, I require you to forbear altogether your Choir-service, so unedifying and offensive: and this as you shall answer it, if any disorder should arise thereupon.

I advise you to catechise, and read and expound the Scripture to the People; not doubting but the Parliament, with the advice of the Assembly of Divines, will advise you farther. I desire your sermons where usually they have been, but more frequent.

Your loving friend,

Oliver Cromwell

The Battle of Marston Moor, fought on the 2nd July 1644, was a great victory for Cromwell's Ironsides, and brought about the ruin of the King's cause in the North.

The place was Marston Fields, which afterwards gave the name to this battle.

Here we drew up our Army. The Enemy was drawn up in Battalia on the Moor a little below us.

The day being, for the most part, spent in preparation we now began to descend toward them.

Lieutenant General Cromwell commanded the Left Wing of Horse; and [was] seconded by Major General Leslie. I had the Right Wing with some Scotch Horse and Lances for my Reserves. The three Generals were with the Foot.

Our Left Wing charged first the Enemy's Right Wing; which was performed for a while with much resolution on both sides; but the Enemy, at length, was put to the worst.

Our Right Wing had not, all, so good success, by reason of the whins and ditches which we were to pass over before we could get to the Enemy, which put us into great disorder: notwithstanding, I drew up a body of 400 Horse. But because the intervals of [their] Horse, in this wing only, were lined with Muskateers; which did us much hurt with their shot: I was necessitated to charge them. We were a long time engaged one with another; but at last we routed that part of their Wing. We charged, and pursued them a good way towards York.

Myself only returned presently, to get to the men I left behind me. But that part of the Enemy which stood [opposite to them], perceiving the disorder they were in, had charged and routed them, before I could get to them. So that the good success we had at first was eclipsed much by this bad conclusion.

But our other Wing, and most of the Foot, went on prosperously till they had cleared the Field.

But I must not forget to remember with thankfulness GOD'S goodness to me this day. For having charged through the Enemy, and my men going after [in] the pursuit; returning back to go to my other troops, I was gotten in among the Enemy, which stood up and down the Field in several bodies of Horse. So, taking the Signal [a white handkerchief] out of my hat, I passed through, for one of their own Commanders; and so got to my Lord of Manchester's Horse in the other Wing; only with a cut in my cheek which was given me in the first charge, and a shot my horse received.

Fairfax's Memorials (? 1665)

After the battle.

Oliver Cromwell, from York, to Colonel Valentine Walton, his brother-in-law. 5th July 1644

It's our duty to sympathise in all mercies; and to praise the Lord together in chastisements or trials, that so we may sorrow together.

Truly England and the Church of God have had a great favour from the Lord, in this great Victory given unto us, such as the like never was seen since this War began. It had all the evidences of an absolute Victory obtained by the Lord's blessing upon the Godly Party principally. We never charged but we routed the enemy. The Left Wing, which I commanded being our own horse saving a few Scots in our rear, beat all the Prince's horse. God made them as stubble to our swords. We charged their regiments of foot with our horse and routed all we charged. The particulars I cannot relate now: but I believe of Twenty Thousand the Prince hath not Four Thousand left. Give glory, all the glory, to God.

Sir, God hath taken away your eldest son by a cannon shot. It brake his leg. We were necessitated to have it cut off, whereof he died.

Sir, you know my own trials this way [Cromwell's son had been killed]: but the Lord supported me with this, That the Lord took him into the happiness we all pant for and live for. There is your precious child full of glory, never to know sin or sorrow any more. He was a gallant young man, exceedingly gracious. God give you His comfort. Before his death he was so full of comfort that to Frank Russel and myself he could not express it, "It was so great above his pain." This he said to us. Indeed it was admirable. A little after he said, One thing lay upon his spirit. I asked him, What that was? He told me it was, that God had not suffered him to be any more the executioner of his enemies. At his fall, his horse being killed with the bullet, and as I am informed three horses more, I am told he bid them, Open to the right and left, that he might see the rogues run. Truly he was exceedingly beloved in the Army of all that knew him. But few knew him; for he was a precious young man, fit for God. You have cause to bless the Lord. He is a glorious Saint in Heaven; wherein you ought exceedingly to rejoice. Let this drink up your sorrow; seeing these are not feigned words to comfort you, but the thing is so real and undoubted a truth. You may do all things by the strength of Christ. Seek that and you shall easily bear your trial. Let this public mercy to the Church of God make you to forget your private sorrow. The Lord be your strength.

The logistics of the War presented formidable problems. The King's headquarters were at Oxford, the most important Royalist garrison and depot, where orders such as the two which follow were constantly being issued.

Order for victuals for garrison at Oxford, 7th June 1644

Whereas we are informed that sufficient care is not taken for the delivery of victuals and provisions to the soldiers of this garrison. It is ordered that Captain Stevens, Commissary General of the Victuals, take special care that provisions be daily made and delivered of bread and cheese according to the usual proportion of one pound in bread and half a pound in cheese to each man. And to that purpose the several Colonels of the respective regiments are to deliver a true list of the number of their common soldiers to the said Commissary that provision may be made accordingly. And the Colonels or Chief Officer of every regiment is desired to take such order that the Quartermasters and officers trusted to receive the provisions for the common soldiers distribute and deliver the same justly and regularly . . .

Order made at Oxford, 27th October 1644

Captain Stevens is hereby required presently to deliver unto Mr. Commissary Pinckney . . . Eight thousand weight of Biscuit (now remaining in His Majesty's stores at the Schools [in Oxford]) to be put up into sacks and laden in carts to be carried away tomorrow, by eight a clock in the morning, towards His Majesty's Army . . .

In February 1645, the Parliamentarian army was remodelled, and Fairfax became General, with Cromwell as Lieutenant-General.

But now I shall come to say something how I came to be engaged in the South.

There being some years spent, in those parts, in a lingering war between the forces of the King and Parliament; and several battles so equally fought as could scarce be known on which side the business in dispute would be determined; though it must be confessed the Parliament's Army was under the command of a very noble and gallant person, the Earl of Essex: yet finding Time and Delay gaining more advantage on their affairs than Force had done; the Parliament resolved to make a change in the constitution of their Army; hoping by it to find a change also in businesses, which were then something in a declining condition.

So as, in this distemper of affairs, the Army was New Modelled, and a new General was proposed to command it. For which, by the votes of the two Houses of Parliament, myself was nominated, though most unfit, and so far from desiring it, that had not so great an authority commanded obedience . . . besides the persuasions of nearest friends . . . I should have "hid myself" [1 Samuel, x. 22] to have avoided so great a charge. But whether it was from a natural facility in me that betrayed my modesty, or the powerful hand of GOD which all things must obey, I was induced to receive the Command.

Fairfax's Memorials (? 1665)

. . . the next question was, Who should be Lord General, and what new officers should be put in or old ones continued? And here the

Parliament House, Westminster Hall and the Abbey

The City of London. C. J. Visscher, 1616

Charles I opening Parliament

Hampden House, Buckinghamshire, the home of John Hampden. The windows were altered and the battlements added c. 1750

New Palace Yard, Westminster

An attack on an ungodly (i.e. Presbyterian) preacher. Wenceslas Hollar

The trial of Strafford in Westminster Hall, 1640. Wenceslas Hollar

A Doctor Vsher, Lord Prim
te of Ireland.
B the Sheriffes of London,
C the Earle of Strafford,
D his kindred and Friends.

The execution of Strafford, 1641. Wenceslas Hollar

Lilburne, smartly whopped at the cart's tail from the Fleet to Westminster, 1638.
From a contemporary Dutch engraving.

The three faces of Laud, Archbishop of Canterbury:
the Bible, the Service Book, Superstition.

The least of these the greatest ought to be;
The other two, of Man and of the Devil,
Ought to be rooted out for e'er as evil.

Laud dining on Prynne's ears

(Two contemporary lampoons)

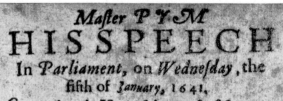

Master *PYM*

HIS SPEECH

In *Parliament*, on *Wednesday*, the
fifth of *January*, 1641.

Concerning the Vote of the House of *Commons*,
for his discharge upon the Accusation of High
Treason, exhibited against himselfe, and the
Lord *Kimbolton* Mr. *Iohn Hampden*, Sr.
Arthur Haslerig, Mr. *Stroud*,
M. *Hollis*, by his Majesty.

London Printed for I.W, 1641.

John Pym, M.P.

Charles attempts to arrest the five members.

Wenceslas Hollar's impression of the scene: the King did not wear his crown, his retinue did not enter the House, the Speaker's chair stood on a dais

The House of Commons in session.   John Glover

Aſſembled at *Weſtminſter*, the thirteenth day of *April*, 1640.

and in the 17 Yeere of his Maieſties happie Raigne.

University of Oxford: the Schools, used by the Royalists as a store for munitions.
D. Loggan

Christ Church, the King's headquarters at Oxford. D. Loggan

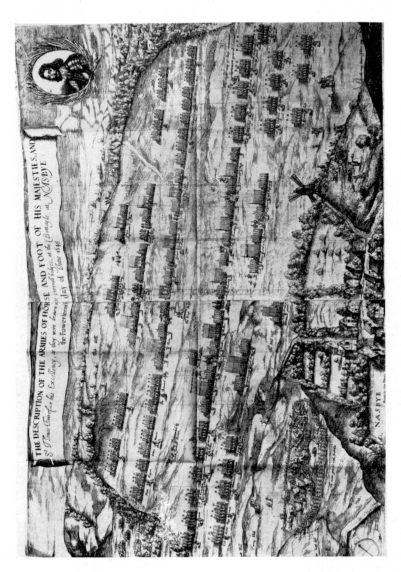

Diagram of the disposition of the armies before the Battle of Naseby

Corfe Castle, slighted by the Parliamentarian forces after its
capture in 1646

Fairfax presiding over the Military Council, 1647

The Great Seal of Charles I

Destruction of the Great Seal

The execution of the King

The Great Seal of the Commonwealth

The Great Seal of the Protectorate. Cromwell replaces Parliament

Cromwell: medal struck to commemorate the victory at
Dunbar, 1650

The SPEECH

WHICH WAS SPOKEN BY

Oliver Cromwell,

When he diffolved the Long Parliament.

IT is high Time for Me to put an End to your Sitting in this Place, which you have difhonoured by your Contempt of all Virtue, and defiled by your Practice of every Vice; Ye are a factious Crew and Enemies to all good Government; Ye are a Pack of mercenary Wretches, and would, like *Efau*, fell your Country for a Mefs of Pottage; and, like *Judas*, betray your GOD for a few Pieces of Money: Is there a fingle Virtue now remaining amongft you? Is there one Vice you do not poffefs? Ye have no more Religion than my Horfe! Gold is your God: Which of you have not bartered your Confcience for Bribes? Is there a Man amongft you that has the leaft Care for the Good of the Common-Wealth? Ye fordid Proftitutes, Have you not defiled this Sacred Place, and turned the LORD's Temple into a Den of Thieves, by your immoral Principles and wicked Practices? Ye are grown intolerably odious to the whole Nation; You were deputed here to get Grievances redreffed; Are not yourfelves become the greateft Grievance? Your Country therefore calls upon me to cleanfe this Augean Stable, by putting a final Period to your iniquitous Procedings in this Houfe;----and which, by God's Help, and the Strength he has given Me, I am now come to do. I command ye, therefore, upon the Peril of your Lives, to depart immediately out of this Place;----Go, get out, make Hafte, ye Venal Slaves, begone! So take away that fhining Bauble there, and lock up the Doors.

Cromwell dissolving the Long Parliament. From a contemporary Dutch engraving

The title-page of *Leviathan*, 1651

Charles II, accepted as King by the Scots — on terms

Edward Hyde, Earl of Clarendon

Charles II

The end of the regicides, and the end of a chapter

policy of Vane and Cromwell did its best: for General they chose Sir Thomas Fairfax, son of the Lord Ferdinando Fairfax, who had been in the wars beyond sea, and had fought valiantly in Yorkshire for the Parliament, though he was overpowered by the Earl of Newcastle's numbers. This man was chosen because they supposed to find him a man of no quickness of parts, of no elocution, of no suspicious plotting wit, and therefore one that Cromwell could make use of at his pleasure. And he was acceptable to sober men because he was religious, faithful, valiant, and of a grave, sober, resolved disposition, very fit for execution and neither too great nor too cunning to be commanded by the Parliament.

RICHARD BAXTER (1615–91), *Reliquiae Baxterianae* (1696)

In the western counties local men banded themselves together into groups of club-men to protect their property against the soldiers of both sides.

Thursday, 3rd July 1645. Fairfax marched from Blandford to Dorchester, 12 miles, a very hot day, where Colonel Sydenham, Governor of Weymouth, gave him information of those parts and of the great danger of Club-men who would not suffer either contributions or victuals to be carried to the Parliamentary garrisons. Mr. Hollis, the Chief Leader of the Club-men . . . affirmed it was fit that the people should shew their grievances and strength. Fairfax treated them civilly . . . for they were so strong at that time that it was held to be a point of prudence to be fair in demeanour towards them for a while.

JOHN RUSHWORTH, *Historical Collections* (1659–1701)

D

The Parliamentarian army was remodelled as a national army under unified control instead of being a collection of county levies, divided in their interests and allegiance. With improved organisation, discipline, equipment, and military skill it swept away the Royalist opposition, so that by the summer of 1646 the King had surrendered to the Scots at Newark, and finally Oxford capitulated. The First Civil War was at an end.

Thomas, Lord Fairfax of Cameron, Lord General of the Parliament Army: when Oxford was surrendered (24 Junii, 1646) the first thing General Fairfax did was to set a good guard of soldiers to preserve the Bodleian Library. 'Tis said there was more hurt done by the cavaliers (during their garrison) by way of embezzling and cutting off chains of books than there was since. He was a lover of learning, and had he not taken this special care, that noble library had been utterly destroyed; for there were ignorant senators enough who would have been contented to have had it so.

JOHN AUBREY (1626–97), *Brief Lives*

CIVILIAN AFFAIRS

Excise, a new system of taxation, was imposed by Parliament in 1643, on ale beer, cider, perry, etc. In 1644 flesh, victuals, salt, caps, hats, silks, stuffs, hops, etc., were added. This tax on food and articles of daily necessity bore especially hardly on the poorer people, who expressed their displeasure by attacking the Excise Office in London. Flesh and salt were removed from the list in 1647.

These two [Salisbury and Silvester] were such pragmatical knaves that they justly became odious to all men; and although necessity might excuse the tax [*i.e.* excise] in other places, yet here it was such a burden that no man of any honesty or conscience could have acted in it. For when plundering troops killed all the poor countrymen's sheep and swine and other provisions, whereby many honest families were ruined and beggared, these unmerciful people would force excise out of them for those very goods which the others had robbed them of.

LUCY HUTCHINSON, *Memoirs of Colonel Hutchinson*
(*c.* 1665; pubd. 1806)

Under an ordinance of 31st March, or 1st April 1643, Parliament gave itself the power to sequestrate the estates of malignants (or Royalists). The wife was entitled to one-fifth of the income from the estate, but frequently she found much difficulty and long delay in obtaining her share.

To the right honourable the Lords in Parliament assembled.
The humble petition of Anne, Countess of Pembroke. July 1644.

Showing that your petitioner having forborne of troubling of your Lordships as long as there was any possibility of substance for her son-in-law the Earl of Thanet, her daughter, his wife, and their children, and therefore out of the affection of a mother to a child your petitioner prayeth leave to present the sad condition of her poor daughter, she having never a bed to lie on but what she hath given security for to be delivered on demand, and she being now in childbed hath not linen or other necessaries for herself or child, the same having been taken from her, and for her 6 children, no means to buy them bread or give them education, her eldest son being at the University of Saumuert [?Saumur in France, though it was not a university] from whence she daily expects to hear he is in prison having no means to maintain him there or to fetch him home . . .

There was often delay, too, in arranging for pardoned Royalists to compound for their offences. Old friendships, suspended but not severed by the War, began to revive again and many former Royalists, now fallen upon hard times, were helped by friends and relations who had fought on the other side.

This year [1646] Sir Allen Apsley, Governor of Barnstaple for the King, after the surrender of that garrison, came and retired to the Governor's house [*i.e.* Colonel Hutchinson's, Governor of Nottingham for the Parliament] till his composition with the Parliament was completed, the Governor's wife being his sister, and the Governor's brother having married the other sister . . . Sir Allen Apsley had not his articles punctually performed, by which he suffered great expense and intolerable vexation . . .

LUCY HUTCHINSON, *Memoirs of Colonel Hutchinson*
(*c.* 1665, pubd. 1806)

This letter also breathes a new tolerance and reasonableness.

Oliver Cromwell, from London, to Thomas Knyvett [a former Royalist]

27th July 1646.

I cannot pretend any interest in you for anything I have done [Cromwell had taken him prisoner at Lowestoft] nor ask any favour for any service I may do you. But because I am conscious to myself of a readiness to serve any gentleman in all possible civilities, I am bold to be beforehand with you to ask your favour on behalf of your honest poor neighbours of Hapton, who, as I am informed, are in some trouble and are likely to be put to more by one Robert Browne, your tenant, who, not well pleased with the way of these men, seeks their disquiet all he may.

Truly nothing moves me to desire this more than the pity I bear them in respect of their honesties and the trouble I hear they are likely to suffer for their consciences. And however the world inter-prets it, I am not ashamed to solicit for such as anywhere are under pressure of this kind, doing even as I would be done by. Sir, this is a quarrelsome age, and the anger seems to me to be the worse where the ground is difference of opinion: which to cure, to hurt men in their names, persons or estates will not be found an apt remedy. Sir, it will not repent you to protect those poor men of Hapton from injury and oppression; which, that you would, is the effect of this letter. Sir, you will not want the grateful acknowledg-ment nor utmost endeavour of requital from

Your most humble servant,

Oliver Cromwell

A courageous Royalist judge.

[David Jenkins] was one of the judges of the Carmarthen, Cardigan, and Pembrokeshire circuits before the wars. In the wars he was taken prisoner at Hereford. Long time prisoner in the Tower, Newgate, Wallingford and Windsor. Never submitted to the usurping power (I think, the only man). All his estate was confiscated; and was always excepted by the Parliament in the first rank of delinquents. In his circuit in Wales at the beginning of the wars he caused to be indicted several men of those parts (that were Parliament, etc., engaged against the King) for high treason; and the grand jury indicted them. Afterwards, when he was a prisoner in Newgate, some of these grandees came to him to triumph over him, and told him that if they had been thus in his power, he would have hanged them. "God forbid else!" replied he — which undaunted return they much admired.

The Parliament intended to have hanged him; and he expected no less, but resolved to be hanged with the Bible under one arm and Magna Carta under the other. And hanged he had been, had not Harry Martin told them in the House that *Sanguis martyrum est semen ecclesiae*, and that that way would do them more mischief. So his life was saved, and they removed him out of the way to Wallingford Castle.

JOHN AUBREY (1626–97), Brief Lives

An honest Parliamentarian judge, Rolle resigned in 1655 rather than take part in proceedings he considered to be unjust.

When I was a student of the Middle Temple from 1646–1656 I many times went to the King's Bench Court and I very well do remember that (although Judge Rolle was of the Parliament party) he never would obey Committee Law: and when Counsel would many times allege the plaintiff or defendant was a Cavalier, he would be peevish at it and say: "What is this to the cause before us?" All who knew him in that station will say that he never warped his administration of justice.

. . . For Serjeant Rolle was just, but by nature penurious; and his wife made him worse.

JOHN AUBREY (1626-97), Brief Lives

Amongst Parliamentarians there were some backsliders.

Lamentable it was to behold how those wretched men fell away . . . not only from public spiritedness but from sobriety and honest, moral conversation: not only conniving at and permitting the wickedness of others but themselves conversing in taverns and brothels, till at last Millington [M.P.] and White were so ensnared that they married a couple of alehouse wenches, to their open shame . . . and some reflection on the Parliament itself, as much as the miscarriage of a Member could cast on it, when Millington, a man of sixty and professing religion and having but lately buried a religious matronly gentlewoman, should go to an alehouse to take a flirtish girl of sixteen.

LUCY HUTCHINSON, Memoirs of Colonel Hutchinson
(c. 1665; pubd. 1806)

Amongst Barking fishwives — and others — religious feelings continued to be strongly and intolerantly expressed.

Depositions taken by Justices of the Peace for the County of Essex

The Information of Robert White of the parish of Barking yeoman taken upon oath the 28th day of June 1645 before Sir Henry

Mildmay, Kt., and William Toppesfeild, Esq., two of His Majesty's Justices of the Peace for the said County.

The informant saith that two months since or thereabouts going along Fishers Street in the town of Barking upon his occasions, Margaret the wife of Thomas Edwards of the same, Fisherman, in a violent and outrageous manner called him roundheaded rogue, and said, It was long of such roundheaded rogues as he was that they were brought into such a condition, using many other reviling words whereby a great tumult was raised in the said town, insomuch that this Informant was constrained to take a marsh fork from a Marshman to defend himself from hurt and violence, which was like to be offered to this Informant by reason of the said uproar and tumult.

The Information of Edmund Palmer of Barking, Draper, taken upon oath *ut supra*.

The Informant saith that about two months since or thereabouts he being then Constable, and going to demand of Thomas Edwards of Barking, Fisherman, some money due upon a rate, Margaret the wife of the said Edwards said to this Informant, *videlicet*, That a company of you had brought a Popish Priest to town, but (saith she) "The King is a-coming now, and then we shall have a course taken with you and such as you are", or words to the like effect.

The Information of Nicholas Cleere of Barking, Mealman, taken upon oath *ut supra*.

Who saith that this day sevennight, going out of the Market, he heard Margaret the wife of the said Thomas Edwards say, That Mr Peter Witham, Preacher of Barking, placed there by the Parliament with the approbation of the Assembly of Divines, was a Papist dog. And further said that if she had been there (meaning at the burial of one Margaret Spence) she would have helped to have torn him in pieces like a Papist dog as he was.

"Stone walls do not a prison make
Nor iron bars a cage."

Colonel Richard Lovelace, Cavalier poet, 1618–58.

James Thompson to Henry Oxinden, 26th October 1648

. . . News to you I believe it may be that Colonel Lovelace is sent to Peterhouse in Aldersgate. The reason and manner of it (as I am told) thus. Search was made for Frank Lovelace in his lodging, who not being found instantly, the Colonel that was employed imagined he might be concealed (I think) in his brother's cabinet, and commanded the violation of that, where a discovery was made of divers Delinquent Jewels. Them they forthwith seized on as Prisoners. Dick, incensed at so great a loss, takes upon him stiffly to argue property, a note which it must be supposed they could not digest when it was in order to disgorging a prize and therefore instantly packed him to Peterhouse, upon pretence of answering some matters contained in papers of his; but his Treasure was ordered to a more private prison. When the day of redemption of either will dawn, we are yet to expect . . .

POLITICAL DEBATE

It was one thing to win a war, but another to settle the government of the country on a stable and generally acceptable basis. The victorious side was united in opposition to Charles but at variance on many other issues.

The King surrendered himself to the Scots at Newark in May 1646. Finding it impossible to come to terms with him they handed him over to Parliament in February 1647, and there followed protracted negotiations between Parliament and the King about his restoration, negotiations that were frustrated by mutual suspicion. Meanwhile another body began to intervene actively in political affairs — the Army, who had won the war, whose pay was seriously in arrear, and who had no intention of being left out whilst King and Parliament patched things up to their private satisfaction. So the soldiers elected agents (known as agitators) to represent their views. Broadly, the Army was for religious tolerance and a democracy whilst Parliament was for Presbyterianism and an oligarchy.

But, how ill deserving so ever we were, yet still it pleased GOD to give the Army success in the years '45 and '46 that there remained in England neither army nor fortress to oppose the Parliament in settling the peace of the Kingdom.

But this shining mercy soon became clouded with the mists of abominable hypocrisy [and] deceit, even in those men who had been instrumental in bringing this War to a conclusion. Here was the vertical point on which the Army's honour and reputation turned into reproach and scandal. Here the power of the Army, which I once had, was usurped by the Forerunners of Confusion and Anarchy, viz., the Agitators.

. . . I shall descend to some particulars of their agitation:

At Nottingham was the first time I took notice of it, by the soldiers' meetings to frame a Petition to the Parliament about their arrears. The thing seemed just: but, not liking the way, I spake with some officers that were principally engaged in it, and got it suppressed for that time.

Which was but as the cutting off of Hydra's head, which soon sprang up again (though not so near the Head Quarters, but in more remote corners of the Army, which I could not so timely prevent) so that they presented it to the Parliament, which they were highly displeased with. And now falling into difference[s] the consequences of which proved fatal not only to the King, but also destructive to one another . . . This (with a natural inclination to change) I believe created the thoughts of a New Government, which in time attained the name of a Common Wealth, though it never arrived to the perfection of it, being sometimes Democratical, sometimes Oligarchical, lastly Anarchical — as indeed all the ways attaining to it seemed nothing but a confusion.

For now the officers of the Army were placed and displaced by the will of the Agitators; who, with violence, so carried all things as it was above my power to restrain it.

Fairfax's Memorials (? 1665)

The Army, exasperated by Parliament, kidnapped the King out of Parliament's custody and opened negotiations with him. The Army put some Proposals to Charles; they displeased him greatly.

HEADS OF PROPOSALS OFFERED BY THE ARMY, 1st AUGUST 1647

. . . .

I. (5) That the elections of the Commons for succeeding Parliaments may be distributed to all counties, or other parts or divisions of the kingdom, according to some rule of equality or proportion, so as all counties may have a number of Parliament members allowed to their choice, proportionable to the respective rates they bear in the common charges and burdens of the kingdom, according to some other rule of equality or proportion, to render the House of Commons (as near as may be) an equal representative of the whole; and in order thereunto, that a present consideration be had to take off the elections of burgesses for poor decayed or inconsiderable towns, and to give some present addition to the number of Parliament members for great counties that have now less than their due proportion, to bring all (at present), as near as may be, to such a rule of proportion as aforesaid.

.   .   .   .

II.   (1) That the power of the militia by sea and land, during the space of ten years next ensuing, shall be ordered and disposed by the Lords and Commons assembled and to be assembled in the Parliament or Parliaments of England, by such persons as they shall nominate and appoint for that purpose from time to time during the said space.

(2) That the said power shall not be ordered, disposed or exercised by the King's Majesty that now is, or by any person or persons by any authority derived from him, during the said space, or at any time hereafter by His said Majesty, without the advice and consent of the said Lords and Commons, or of such Committees or Council in the intervals of Parliament as they shall appoint.

.   .   .   .

III.   (4) That there be a Council of State, with power to superintend and direct the several and particular powers of the militia last mentioned, for the peace and safety of this kingdom and of Ireland.

(5) That the same Council may have power as the King's Privy Council, for and in all foreign negotiations; provided that the making of war or peace with any other kingdom or state shall not be without the advice and consent of Parliament.

(6) That the said power of the Council of State be put into the hands of trusty and able persons now to be agreed on and the same persons to continue in that power (*si bene se gesserint*) for the certain term not exceeding seven years.

. . . .

XI.   An Act to be passed to take away all coercive power, authority, and jurisdiction of Bishops and all other Ecclesiastical Officers whatsoever, extending to any civil penalties upon any: and to repeal all laws whereby the civil magistracy hath been, or is bound, upon any ecclesiastical censure to proceed (*ex officio*) unto any civil penalties against any persons so censured.

XII.   That there be a repeal of all Acts or clauses in any Act enjoining the use of the Book of Common Prayer, and imposing any penalties for neglect thereof; as also of all Acts or clauses of any Act, imposing any penalty for not coming to church, or for meetings elsewhere for prayer or other religious duties, exercises or ordinances, and some other provision to be made for discovering of Papists and Popish recusants, and for disabling of them, and of all Jesuits or priests from disturbing the State.

. . . .

Next to the Proposals aforesaid for the present settling of a peace, we shall desire that no time may be lost by the Parliament for despatch of other things tending to the welfare, ease and just satisfaction of the kingdom, and in special manner:

. . . .

V.   That provision may be made for payment of arrears to the army, and the rest of the soldiers of the kingdom who have concurred with the army in the late desires and proceedings thereof; and in the next place for payment of the public debts and damages of the kingdom; and that to be performed, first to such persons whose debt or damages (upon the public account) are great, and their estates small, so as they are thereby reduced to a difficulty of subsistence: . . . .

In October, five Regiments, dissatisfied with the lack of progress, elected new agitators, more extreme men known as Levellers, by whom this democratic document was drawn up.

THE AGREEMENT OF THE PEOPLE, AS PRESENTED TO THE ARMY, 28th OCTOBER 1647

An Agreement of the People for a firm and present peace upon grounds of common right.

Having by our late labours and hazards made it appear to the world at how high a rate we value our just freedom, and God having so far owned our cause as to deliver the enemies thereof into our hands, we do now hold ourselves bound in mutual duty to each other to take the best care we can for the future to avoid both the danger of returning into a slavish condition and the chargeable remedy of another war; for, as it cannot be imagined that so many of our countrymen would have opposed us in this quarrel if they had understood their own good, so may we safely promise to ourselves that, when our common rights and liberties shall be cleared, their endeavours will be disappointed that seek to make themselves our masters. Since, therefore, our former oppressions and scarce-yet-ended troubles have been occasioned, either by want of frequent national meetings in Council, or by rendering those meetings ineffectual, we are fully agreed and resolved to provide that hereafter our representatives be neither left to an uncertainty for the time nor made useless to the ends for which they are intended. In order whereunto we declare:—

I

That the people of England, being at this day very unequally distributed by Counties, Cities, and Boroughs for the election of their deputies in Parliament, ought to be more indifferently proportioned according to the number of the inhabitants; the circumstances whereof for number, place, and manner are to be set down before the end of this present Parliament.

II

That, to prevent the many inconveniences apparently arising from the long continuance of the same persons in authority, this present Parliament be dissolved upon the last day of September which shall be in the year of our Lord 1648.

III   *114383*

That the people do, of course, choose themselves a Parliament once in two years, viz. upon the first Thursday in every 2d. March, after the manner as shall be prescribed before the end of this Parliament, to begin to sit upon the first Thursday in April following at Westminster or such other place as shall be appointed from time to time by the preceding Representatives, and to continue till the last day of September then next ensuing, and no longer.

IV

That the power of this, and all future Representatives of this Nation, is inferior only to theirs who choose them, and doth extend, without the consent or concurrence of any other person or persons, to the enacting, altering, and repealing of laws, to the erecting and abolishing of offices and courts, to the appointing, removing, and calling to account magistrates and officers of all degrees, to the making war and peace, to the treating with foreign States, and, generally, to whatsoever is not expressly or impliedly reserved by the represented to themselves:

Which are as followeth.

1. That matters of religion and the ways of God's worship are not at all entrusted by us to any human power, because therein we cannot remit or exceed a title of what our consciences dictate to be the mind of God without wilful sin: nevertheless the public way of instructing the nation (so it be not compulsive) is referred to their discretion.

2. That the matter of impresting and constraining any of us to serve in the wars is against our freedom; and therefore we do not

allow it in our Representatives; the rather, because money (the sinews of war), being always at their disposal, they can never want numbers of men apt enough to engage in any just cause.

3.   That after the dissolution of this present Parliament, no person be at any time questioned for anything said or done in reference to the late public differences, otherwise than in execution of the judgments of the present Representatives or House of Commons.

4.   That in all laws made or to be made every person may be bound alike, and that no tenure, estate, charter, degree, birth or place do confer any exemption from the ordinary course of legal proceedings whereunto others are subjected.

5.   That as the laws ought to be equal, so they must be good, and not evidently destructive to the safety and well-being of the people.

These things we declare to be our native rights, and therefore are agreed and resolved to maintain them with our utmost possibilities against all opposition whatsoever; being compelled thereunto not only by the examples of our ancestors, whose blood was often spent in vain for the recovery of their freedoms, suffering themselves through fraudulent accommodations to be still deluded of the fruit of their victories, but also by our own woeful experience, who, having long expected and dearly earned the establishment of these certain rules of government, are yet made to depend for the settlement of our peace and freedom upon him that intended our bondage and brought a cruel war upon us.

In late October and early November 1647, the Council of the Army met at Putney with two officers and two agitators from each regiment to debate the Agreement of the People, and the question of what should be done. These few extracts from speeches made during the debate vividly illustrate the profound division on fundamental political principles.

Colonel Thomas Rainborough . . . For really I think that the poorest he that is in England hath a life to live, as the greatest he; and therefore truly, Sir, I think it's clear that every man that is to

live under a government ought first by his own consent to put
himself under that government; and I do think that the poorest
man in England is not at all bound in a strict sense to that government that he hath not had a voice to put himself under . . .

   Commissary-General Ireton . . . if you make this rule I think you
must fly for refuge to an absolute natural right, and you must deny
all civil right . . . For my part I think it is no right at all. I think
that no person hath a right to an interest or share in the disposing
of the affairs of the Kingdom, and in determining or choosing those
that shall determine what laws we shall be ruled by here — no
person hath a right to this that hath not a permanent fixed interest
in this Kingdom, and those persons together are properly the represented of this Kingdom, and consequently are to make up the representers of this Kingdom . . . That by a man's being born here he
shall have a share in that power that shall dispose of the lands here,
and of all things here, I do not think it a sufficient ground . . .
those that choose the representers for the making of laws by which
this State and Kingdom are to be governed are . . . the persons in
whom all land lies, and those in corporations in whom all trading
lies. This is the most fundamental constitution of this Kingdom . . .

   Rainborough . . . I do hear nothing at all that can convince me
why any man that is born in England ought not to have his voice in
election of burgesses [of Parliament]. It is said if a man have not a
permanent interest he can have no claim; and that we must be no
freer than the laws will let us be, and that there is no law in any
chronicle will let us be freer than what we now enjoy. Something
was said to this yesterday. I do think that the main cause why Almighty God gave men reason, it was that they should make use of
that reason . . .

   Ireton . . . All the main thing that I speak for, is because I would
have an eye to property . . . let every man consider with himself
that he do not go that way to take away all property. For here is
the case of the most fundamental part of the constitution of the
Kingdom, which if you take away, you take away all by that . . .
I wish we may all consider of what right you will challenge that all

the people should have a right to elections. Is it by the right of nature? If you will have forth that as your ground, then I think you must deny all property too, and this is my reason. For thus: by that same right of nature (whatever it be) that you pretend, by which you can say, one man hath an equal right with another to the choosing of him that shall govern him — by the same right of nature he hath the same equal right in any goods he sees — meat, drink, clothes — to take and use them for his sustenance. He hath a freedom to take to the land, to exercise it, till it; he hath the same freedom to anything that anyone doth account himself to have any propriety in . . .

Rainborough . . . Sir, to say that because a man pleads that every man hath a voice by right of nature, that therefore it destroys by the same argument all property — this is to forget the Law of God. That there is a property, the Law of God says it; else why hath God made that law, *Thou shalt not steal?* . . . For my part I am against any such thought that property is wrong and I wish you would not make the world believe that we are for anarchy.

Mr Maximilian Petty . . . as for this argument, that it destroys all right to property that every Englishman that is an inhabitant of England should choose and have a voice in the representatives, I suppose it is, on the contrary, the only means to preserve all property. For I judge every man is naturally free; and I judge the reason why men chose representatives . . . was that those who were chosen might preserve property for all; and therefore men agreed to come into some form of government that they might preserve property . . .

Colonel Nathaniel Rich . . . If the master and servant shall be equal electors, then clearly those that have no interest in the Kingdom will make it their interest to choose those that have no interest. It may then happen that the majority may by law destroy property; there may be a law enacted that there shall be an equality of goods and estate. I think that either of the extremes may be urged to inconveniency; that is, that men that have no interest as to estate should have no interest as to election, or that they should have an equal interest. But there may be a more equitable division and distribution than that he that hath nothing should have an equal voice; and certainly there may be some other way thought of, that there may be a representative of the poor as well as the rich, and not to exclude all . . .

Ireton. Let the question be so: Whether a man can be bound to any law that he doth not consent to? And I shall tell you that he may and ought to be . . .

Mr Edward Sexby (an agitator appointed by Fairfax's Regiment of Horse). I see that though liberty were our end, there is a degeneration from it. We have engaged in this Kingdom and ventured our lives, and it was all for this: to recover our birthrights and privileges as Englishmen; and by the arguments used there is none. There are many thousands of us soldiers, that have ventured our lives; we have had little propriety in the Kingdom as to our estates, yet we have had a birthright. But it seems now, except a man hath a fixed estate in this Kingdom, he hath no right in this Kingdom. I wonder we were so much deceived . . .

Arrears of pay: a standing grievance of the Army.

Tuesday, 23rd November 1647. A letter this day from Bristol informing the House [of Commons] that the soldiers there had secured an Alderman of that City and would not discharge him until they had a months pay and an ordinance of indemnity for the act.

The House hereupon ordered a letter to be sent to His Excellency [Fairfax] to desire him to give order forthwith for the discharge of the said Alderman and give directions to prevent the like abuses for the future by the soldiers there.

JOHN RUSHWORTH, *Historical Collections* (1659–1701)

*In December 1648, the Council of Officers met at Whitehall to debate
the question whether the government should have any powers in matters
of religion. The debate was inconclusive, and, to Lt.-Col. John Lilburne,
the Leveller, unsatisfactory.*

. . . For when it came to the Council, there came the General,
Cromwell, and the whole gang of creature-Colonels and other
officers, and spent many days in taking it all in pieces, and there
Ireton showed himself an absolute king, if not an emperor, against
whose will no man must dispute. And then shuttlecock Roe, their
scout, Okey, and Major Barton (where Sir Hardress Waller sat
president) begun in their open council to quarrel with us by giving
some of us base and unworthy language; which procured them
from me a sharp retortment of their own baseness and unworthiness
into their teeth, and a challenge from myself into the field besides . . .
And within a little time after I took my leave of them for a pack of
dissembling, juggling knaves amongst whom in consultation ever
thereafter I should scorn to come (as I told some of them) for there
was neither faith, truth nor common honesty amongst them.

JOHN LILBURNE, *Legal Fundamental Liberties* (1649)

Political equality was the Leveller creed.

. . . Adam . . . and . . . Eve . . . are the earthly original fountain
of all and every particular and individual man and woman in the
world since, who are, and were, by nature all equal and alike in
power, dignity, authority, and majesty, none of them having by
nature, dominion or magisterial power one over or above another;
neither have they, or can they exercise any, but merely by insti-
tution or donation, or assumed by mutual consent and agreement . . .
And unnatural, irrational, sinful, wicked, unjust, devilish, and
tyrannical, it is for any man whatsoever, spiritual or temporal,
clergyman or layman, to appropriate and assume unto himself a
power, authority, and jurisdiction to rule, govern or reign over any

sort of man in the world without their free consent, and whosoever doth it . . . do thereby, as much as in them lies, endeavour to appropriate and assume unto themselves the office and sovereignty of God (who alone doth, and is to, rule by his will and pleasure) and to be like the Creator, which was the sin of the devils, not being content with their first station, would be like God, for which sin they were thrown down into Hell . . .

JOHN LILBURNE, *The Free-man's Freedom Vindicated* (1646)

Lilburne might be a Leveller and a democrat, but he was also conscious of his gentility.

Divers of the prisoners at Oxford were arraigned [1643] and amongst the rest Captain John Lilburne, indicted by the name of John Lilburne, yeoman, for High Treason . . . He would not plead to that indictment, as it was drawn, for he would not have anything on record so much to the prejudice of his family (who were gentlemen and had continued ever since William the Conqueror in the Bishopric of Durham) as to answer to the name of yeoman . . . Whereupon Judge Heath ordered the record to be amended . . . He was afterwards found guilty, but upon the Parliament's declaration . . . threatening *Lex talionis*, reprieved, and so in time exchanged and got his liberty.

JOHN RUSHWORTH, *Historical Collections* (1659–1701)

The Diggers went further than the Levellers in their demand for equality, and believed in communal ownership of property. The digging-up of St. George's Hill did not get far. Only a dozen or so men took part in it, and after a few months the authorities put an end to their activities.

In the beginning of time, the great Creator, Reason, made the earth to be a common treasury, to preserve beasts, birds, fishes, and man, the Lord that was to govern this creation. For man had domination given to him over the beasts, birds and fishes. But not one word was spoken in the beginning, that one branch of mankind should rule over another.

And the reason is this. Every single man, male and female, is a perfect creature of himself. And the same Spirit that made the globe dwells in man to govern the globe; so that the flesh of man, being subject to Reason, his Maker, hath him to be his teacher and ruler within himself, therefore needs not run abroad after any teacher and ruler without him . . .

But since human flesh . . . began to delight himself in the objects of the creation more than in the Spirit, Reason and Righteousness, who manifests himself to be the indweller in the five senses . . . ; then he fell into blindness of mind and weakness of heart, and runs abroad for a teacher and ruler, and so selfish imaginations, taking possession of the five senses, and ruling as king in the room of Reason therein, and working with covetousness, did set up one man to teach and rule over another. And thereby the Spirit was killed, and man was brought into bondage and became a greater slave to such of his own kind than the beasts of the field were to him.

And hereupon the earth, which was made to be a common treasury of relief to all, both beasts and men, was hedged into enclosures by the teachers and rulers, and the others were made servants and slaves. And that earth that is within this creation made a common storehouse for all, is bought and sold and kept in the hands of a few; whereby the great Creator is mightily dishonoured: as if he were a respecter of persons, delighting in the comfortable livelihood of some, and rejoicing in the miserable poverty and straits of others. From the beginning it was not so . . .

But for the present state of the old world, that is running up like parchment in the fire and wearing away, we see proud imaginary flesh, which is the wise serpent, rises up in flesh and gets dominion in some to rule over others, and so forces one part of the creation, man, to be a slave to another. And thereby the Spirit is killed in both. The one looks upon himself as a teacher and ruler, and so is lifted up in pride over his fellow creature. The other looks upon himself as imperfect, and so is dejected in his spirit, and looks upon his fellow creature, of his own image, as a lord above him.

. . . .

But when once the earth becomes a common treasury again — as it must; for all the prophecies of scriptures and reason are circled here in this community, and mankind must have the law of righteousness once more writ in his heart, and all must be made of one heart and one mind — then this enmity in all lands will cease. For none shall dare to seek a dominion over others; neither shall any dare to kill another, nor desire more of the earth than another. For he that will rule over, imprison, oppress, and kill his fellow creatures under what pretence soever, is a destroyer of the creation and an actor of the curse, and walks contrary to the rule of righteousness: Do as you would have others do to you; and love your enemies, not in words, but in actions.

Therefore you powers of the earth, or Lord Esau, the elder brother, because you have appeared to rule the creation, first take notice that the power that sets you to work is selfish covetousness, and an aspiring pride to live in glory and ease over Jacob, the meek spirit; that is, the seed that lies hid in and among the poor common people, or younger brother, out of whom the blessing of deliverance is to rise and spring up to all nations. And Reason, the living King of Righteousness, doth only look on and lets thee alone, that whereas thou counts thyself an angel of light, thou shalt appear in the light of the Sun to be a devil . . . and the curse that the creation groans under. And the time is now come for thy downfall; and Jacob must rise, who is the universal spirit of love and righteousness that fills, and will fill, all the earth . . .

. . . .

The work we are going about is this: to dig up George's Hill and the waste ground thereabouts, and to sow corn, and to eat our bread together by the sweat of our brows.

And the first reason is this. That we may work in righteousness, and lay the foundation of making the earth a common treasury for all, both rich and poor. That every one that is born in the land may be fed by the earth, his mother that brought him forth, according to the reason that rules in the creation, not enclosing any part into any particular hand, but all as one man working together, and feeding together as sons of one father, members of one family; not one lording over another, but all looking upon each other as equals in the creation. So that our Maker may be glorified in the work of his hands, and that every one may see he is no respecter of persons, but equally loves his whole creation, and hates nothing but the serpent. Which is covetousness, branching forth into selfish imagination, pride, envy, hypocrisy, uncleanness, all seeking the ease and honour of flesh, and fighting against the Spirit Reason that made the creation. For that is the corruption, the curse, the devil, the father of lies, death and bondage — that serpent and dragon that the creation is to be delivered from.

And we are moved hereunto for that reason, and others which hath been showed us, both by vision, voice, and revelation. For it is showed us, that so long as we or any other doth own the earth to be the peculiar interest of lords and landlords, and not common to others as well as them, we own the curse that holds the creation under bondage. And so long as we or any other doth own landlords and tenants, for one to call the land his, or another to hire it of him, or for one to give hire, and for another to work for hire; this is to dishonour the work of creation — as if the righteous Creator should have respect to persons, and therefore made the earth for some, and not for all . . .

And that this civil propriety is the curse, is manifest thus. Those that buy and sell land and are landlords, have got it either by oppression or murder or theft; and all landlords live in the breach of the Seventh and Eighth Commandments, Thou shalt not steal, nor kill.

The True Leveller's Standard Advanced (1649)

IDEAS ABOUT FREEDOM AND LIBERTY

14 June 1643. It is therefore ordered by the Lords and Commons in Parliament that no book, pamphlet or paper shall from henceforth be printed, bound, stitched or put to sale by any person or persons whatsoever, unless the same be first approved of and licensed under the hands of such person or persons as Both or either of the said Houses shall appoint . . .

A speech for the liberty of unlicensed printing to the Parliament of England.

. . . if therefore ye be loth to dishearten heartily and discontent, not the mercenary crew of false pretenders to learning, but the free and ingenuous sort of such as evidently were born to study, and love learning for itself, not for lucre or any other end but the service of God and of truth, and perhaps that lasting fame and perpetuity of praise which God and good men have consented shall be the reward of those whose published labours advance the good of mankind, then know that, so far to distrust the judgment and the honesty of one who hath but a common repute in learning, and never yet offended, as not to count him fit to print his mind without a tutor and examiner, lest he should drop a schism or something of corruption, is the greatest displeasure and indignity to a free and knowing spirit that can be put upon him.

.   .   .   .

I fear yet this iron yoke of outward conformity hath left a slavish print upon our necks; the ghost of a linen decency yet haunts us . . . We do not see that, while we still affect by all means a rigid external formality, we may as soon fall again into a gross conforming stupidity, a stark and dead congealment of wood and hay and stubble forced and frozen together . . .

JOHN MILTON, *Areopagitica* (1644)

THE CHARACTER OF MILTON

His harmonical and ingenious soul did lodge in a beautiful and well-proportioned body. He was a spare man. He was scarce so tall as I am — *quaere, quot* feet I am high: *resp.*, of middle stature. He had auburn hair. His complexion exceeding fair — he was so fair that they called him "the lady of Christ's College". Oval face. His eye a dark grey. He had a delicate, tuneable voice and had good skill. His father instructed him. He had an organ in his house: he played on that most. Of a very cheerful humour. He would be cheerful even in his gout-fits, and sing. He was very healthy and free from all diseases: seldom took any physic (only sometimes he took manna): only towards his latter end he was visited with gout, spring and fall. He had a very good memory; but I believe that his excellent method of thinking and disposing did much to help his memory . . .

His exercise was chiefly walking. He was an early riser (*scil.* at 4 a clock *mane*); yea, after he lost his sight. He had a man to read to him. The first thing he read was the Hebrew Bible, and that was at 4h. *mane* $\frac{1}{2}$ h. or so. Then he contemplated. At 7 his man came to him again, and then read to him again and wrote till dinner: the writing was as much as the reading. His daughter Deborah could read to him Latin, Italian, and French, and Greek . . .

After dinner he used to walk three or four hours at a time (he always had a garden where he lived); went to bed about 9. Temperate man, rarely drank between meals. Extreme pleasant in his conversation, and at dinner, supper, etc.; but satirical.

JOHN AUBREY (1626–97), *Brief Lives*

Mr. Bendish has heard the widow or daughter or both say it, that soon after the Restoration the King offered to employ this pardoned man as his Latin Secretary, the post in which he served Cromwell with so much integrity and ability: (that a like offer was made to Thurlow is not disputed as ever I heard). Milton withstood the offer; the wife pressed his compliance. "Thou art in the

right" (says he) "You, as other women, would ride in your coach;
for me, my aim is to live and die an honest man."

J. RICHARDSON, *Explanatory Notes and Remarks on Paradise
Lost, with the life of the Author* (pubd. 1724)

A PLEA FOR TOLERATION OF RELIGIOUS
BELIEF

Let there be free debates and open conferences and communica-
tion, for all and of all sorts that will, concerning differences in spirituals; still allowing the state to secure all tumult or disturbances.
Where doors are not shut, there will be no breaking them open.
So where debates are free there is a way of vent and evacuation,
the stopping of which hath caused more troubles in states than
anything; for where there is much new wine in old bottles the
working will be such as the parable speaks on . . .

Let us not, being under no further degree of the revelation of
truth and coming out of Babylon, assume any power of infallibility
to each other . . . for there lies as much on one side for compulsion
as another, respectively to one another, for another's evidence is as
dark to me as mine to him, and mine to him as his to me, till the
Lord enlighten us both for discerning alike. So when there is no
power in us to make that appear to another which appears to us,
there can be no reasonable equity for any enforcing or compelling
in spirituals . . .

Let not those believers who have the advantage of the magistrate
strive to make any unwarrantable use of it one against another,
because scripture principles are not so clear for it; and because they
know not the resolution of Providence, and we are to do as we would
be done to . . .

Consider that we may be one in Christ though we think diversely,
and we may be friends though not brethren, and let us attain to
union though not to unity.

JOHN SALTMARSH, *Smoke in the Temple* (1646)

LIBERTY A DIVINE GIFT

Give then to Caesar the things that are Caesar's . . . Our liberty is not Caesar's. It is a blessing we have received from God himself. It is what we are born to. To lay this down at Caesar's feet, which we derive not from him, which we are not beholden to him for, were an unworthy action, and a degrading of our very nature. If one should consider attentively the countenance of a man, and inquire after whose image so noble a creature were framed, would not any one that did so presently make answer that he was made after the image of God himself? Being therefore peculiarly God's own, that is, truly free, we are consequently to be subjected to him alone, and cannot, without the greatest sacrilege imaginable, be reduced into a condition of slavery to any man, especially to a wicked, unjust, cruel tyrant . . . Absolute lordship and Christianity are inconsistent.

JOHN MILTON, Pro Populo Anglicano Defensio (1651)

For Hobbes, unlike Milton, politics were not a question of morality but of expediency. He came into the world at the time of the Spanish Armada ("Fear and I were born in one hour" as he said), a circumstance which he offered as an explanation of his unvaliant disposition. To avoid the mounting troubles in England he withdrew to France in 1640 and for a time was mathematical tutor to the future Charles II. His Leviathan, *one of the greatest works of political theory in the English language, was published in London in 1651. His thesis, a vindication of the absolute rights of whatever government happens to be in power, was scarcely compatible with the Stuart doctrine of the Divine right of Kings, and Hobbes's presentation of a specially written and bound copy of* Leviathan *to Charles after his escape from Worcester in 1651 was, to say the least, tactless. Shortly afterwards he returned to England, naively believing that the doctrine of* Leviathan *would appeal to Cromwell. His religious opinions were even more unorthodox than his political theories, but he was allowed to live quietly during the Interregnum, and even returned to a modicum of royal favour after the Restoration.*

... the condition of Man ... is a condition of War of everyone against everyone ... [that is, at a] time wherein men live without other security than what their own strength and their own invention shall furnish them withal. In such a condition there is no place for Industry, because the fruit thereof is uncertain; and consequently no culture of the earth, no navigation, nor use of the commodities that may be imported by sea ... no arts, no letters, no society; and which is worst of all, continual fear and danger of violent death; and the life of man, solitary, poor, nasty, brutish, and short ...

The final cause, end, or design of men (who naturally love liberty, and dominion over others) in the introduction of that restraint upon themselves (in which we see them live in commonwealths), is the foresight of their own preservation, and of a more contented life thereby; that is to say, of getting themselves out from that miserable condition of War, which is necessarily consequent to the natural passions of men when there is no visible Power to keep them in awe, and tie them by fear of punishment to the performance of their covenants, and observation of [the] Laws of Nature ...

For the Laws of Nature (as Justice, Equity, Modesty, Mercy), and, in sum, *doing to others as we would be done to* of themselves, without the terror of some Power to cause them to be observed, are contrary to our natural passions ... And covenants, without the sword, are but words ...

The only way to erect such a Common Power ... is to confer all their power and strength upon one man, or one assembly of men ... and to submit their wills, everyone to his will, and their judgments, everyone to his judgment ... He that carrieth this Person is called Sovereign and said to have Sovereign Power; and everyone besides, his Subject ...

But a man may here object that the condition of subjects is very miserable ... not considering that the estate of Man can never be without some incommodity or other, and that the greatest that in any form of Government can possibly happen to the people in general is scarce sensible, in respect of the miseries and horrible calamities that accompany a Civil War ...

THOMAS HOBBES, *Leviathan* (1651)

THE CHARACTER OF HOBBES

The Lord Chancellor Bacon loved to converse with him [Hobbes]. He assisted his lordship in translating several of his essays into Latin . . . His lordship was a very contemplative person, and was wont to contemplate in his delicious walks at Gorhambury, and dictate to Mr Thomas Bushell, or some others of his gentlemen that attended him with ink and paper ready to set down presently his thoughts. His lordship would often say he better liked Mr Hobbes's taking his thoughts than any of the other, because he understood what he wrote, which the others not understanding, my Lord would many times have a hard task to make sense of what they writ.

. . . .

In his old age he was very bald (which claimed a veneration), yet within door he used to study, and sit, bare-headed, and said he never took cold in his head, but that the greatest trouble was to keep off the flies from pitching on his baldness . . . He thought much and with excellent method and steadiness, which made him seldom make a false step.

. . . .

He had always books of prick-song lying on his table — *e.g.* of H. Lawes', etc. *Songs* — which at night, when he was abed, and the doors made fast, and was sure nobody heard him, he sang aloud (not that he had a very good voice) but for his health's sake: he did believe it did his lungs good and conduced much to prolong his life. [He died in 1679, aged 91.]

JOHN AUBREY (1626–97), *Brief Lives*

THE EXECUTION OF CHARLES I

A YEAR EARLIER

Oliver Cromwell, from Putney, to Colonel Whalley,
November 1647

There are rumours abroad of some intended attempt on His
Majesty's person. Therefore I pray have a care of your guards. If
any such thing should be done, it would be counted a most horrid
act . . .

*The Army was embittered by the renewed outbreak of war in 1648, and
exasperated by the tergiversations of Parliament and the repeatedly
demonstrated unreliability and insincerity of Charles. On the 6th December, Colonel Pride, on the direction of Ireton and other officers, adjourned
to Parliament, which contrary to its own earlier decisions continued to
negotiate with the King, and Pride purged the Commons of one hundred
and forty three Presbyterian members, leaving a "Rump" of about fifty
or sixty, who were determined to bring the King to trial. The Lords refused
to pass the ordinance setting up a court to try the King, but the Rump
nevertheless went ahead. Of the one hundred and thirty five commissioners
appointed to constitute the court only about one half could be persuaded
to act.*

THE ORDINANCE SETTING UP A COURT TO
TRY THE KING, 6th JANUARY 1648/9

Whereas it is notorious that Charles Stuart, the now King of England, not content with the many encroachments which his predecessors had made upon the people in their rights and freedom, hath had a wicked design totally to subvert the ancient and fundamental laws and liberties of this nation, and in their place to introduce an arbitrary and tyrannical government, and that besides all other evil ways and means to bring his design to pass, he hath prosecuted it with fire and sword, levied and maintained a civil way in the land, against the Parliament and kingdom; whereby this country hath been miserably wasted, the public treasure exhausted, trade decayed, thousands of people murdered, and infinite other mischiefs committed; for all which high and treasonable offences the said Charles Stuart might long since have justly been brought to exemplary and condign punishment: whereas also the Parliament, well hoping that the restraint and imprisonment of his person, after it had pleased God to deliver him into their hands, would have quieted the distempers of the kingdom, did forbear to proceed judicially against him, but found, by sad experience, that such their remissness served only to encourage him and his accomplices in the continuance of their evil practices, and in raising new commotions, rebellions and invasions: for prevention therefore of the like or greater inconveniences, and to the end no Chief Officer or Magistrate whatsoever may hereafter presume, traitorously and maliciously, to imagine or contrive the enslaving or destroying of the English nation, and to expect impunity for so doing; be it enacted and ordained by the (Lords and) Commons in Parliament assembled, and it is hereby enacted and ordained by the authority thereof, that the Earls of Kent, Nottingham, Pembroke, Denbigh and Mulgrave, the Lord Grey of Wark, Lord Chief Justice Rolle of the King's Bench, Lord Chief Justice St. John of the Common Pleas, and Lord Chief Baron Wylde, the Lord Fairfax, Lieutenant-General Cromwell, and others [in all about 135], shall be and are hereby appointed and required to be Commissioners and

Judges for the hearing, trying and judging of the said Charles Stuart; and the said Commissioners, or any twenty or more of them, shall be, and are hereby authorised and constituted an High Court of Justice, to meet and sit at such convenient times and place as by the said Commissioners, or the major part, or twenty or more of them, under their hands and seals, shall be appointed and notified by proclamation in the Great Hall or Palace-Yard of Westminster; and to adjourn from time to time, and from place to place, as the said High Court, or the major part thereof, at meeting shall hold fit; and to take order for the charging of him, the said Charles Stuart, with the crimes and treasons above mentioned, and for receiving his personal answer thereunto, and for examination of witnesses upon oath (which the Court hath hereby authority to administer) or otherwise, and taking any other evidence concerning the same; and thereupon, or in default of such answer, to proceed to final sentence according to justice and the merit of the cause; and such final sentence to execute, or cause to be executed, speedily and impartially.

And the said Court is hereby authorised and required to choose and appoint all such officers, attendants and other circumstances as they, or the major part of them, shall in any sort judge necessary or useful for the orderly and good managing of the premises; and Thomas Lord Fairfax the General, and all officers and soldiers under his command, are hereby authorised and required to be aiding and assisting unto the said Court in the due execution of the trust hereby committed unto them; provided that this Act, and the authority hereby granted, do continue in force for the space of one month from the date of the making thereof, and no longer.

THE CHARGE AGAINST THE KING

That the said Charles Stuart, being admitted King of England, and therein trusted with a limited power to govern by and according to the laws of the land, and not otherwise; and by his trust, oath,

E

and office, being obliged to use the power committed to him for the good and benefit of the people, and for the preservation of their rights and liberties; yet, nevertheless, out of a wicked design to erect and uphold in himself an unlimited and tyrannical power to rule according to his will, and to overthrow the rights and liberties of the people, yea, to take away and make void the foundations thereof, and of all redress and remedy of misgovernment, which by the fundamental constitutions of this kingdom were reserved on the people's behalf in the right and power of frequent and successive Parliaments, or national meetings in Council; he, the said Charles Stuart, for accomplishment of such his designs, and for the protecting of himself and his adherents in his and their wicked practices, to the same ends hath traitorously and maliciously levied war against the present Parliament, and the people therein represented, particularly upon or about the 30th day of June, in the year of our Lord 1642, at Beverley in the County of York; and upon or about the 24th day of August in the same year, at the County of the Town of Nottingham, where and when he set up his standard of war; and also on or about the 23rd day of October in the same year, at Edgehill or Keynton-field, in the County of Warwick; and upon or about the 30th day of November in the same year, at Brentford, in the County of Middlesex; and upon or about the 30th day of August, in the year of our Lord 1643, at the Caversham Bridge, near Reading, in the County of Berks; and upon or about the 30th day of October in the year last mentioned at or upon the City of Gloucester; and upon or about the 30th day of November in the year last mentioned, at Newbury, in the County of Berks; and upon or about the 31st day of July, in the year of our Lord 1644, at Cropredy Bridge, in the County of Oxon; and upon or about the 30th day of September in the last year mentioned, at Bodmin and other places near adjacent, in the County of Cornwall; and upon or about the 30th day of November in the year last mentioned, at Newbury aforesaid; and upon or about the 8th day of June, in the year of our Lord 1645, at the Town of Leicester; and also upon the 14th day of the same month in the same year, at Naseby-field, in the County of Northampton. At which several times and places, or most of them, and at many other places in this land, at several other times within the years aforementioned, and in the year of our Lord 1646, he, the said Charles Stuart, hath caused and procured many thousands of the free people of this nation to be slain; and by divisions, parties, and insurrections within this land, by invasions from foreign parts, endeavoured and procured by him, and by many other evil ways and means, he, the said Charles Stuart, hath not only maintained and carried on the said war both by land and sea, during the years beforementioned, but also hath renewed, or caused to be renewed, the said war against the Parliament and good people of this nation in this present year 1648, in the Counties of Kent, Essex, Surrey, Sussex, Middlesex, and many other Counties and places in England and Wales, and also by sea. And particularly he, the said Charles Stuart, hath for that purpose given commission to his son the Prince, and others, whereby, besides multitudes of other persons, many such as were by the Parliament entrusted and employed for the safety of the nation (being by him or his agents corrupted to the betraying of their trust, and revolting from the Parliament), have had entertainment and commission for the continuing and renewing of war and hostility against the said Parliament and people as aforesaid. By which cruel and unnatural wars, by him, the said Charles Stuart, levied, continued, and renewed as aforesaid, much innocent blood of the free people of this nation hath been spilt, many families have been undone, the public treasure wasted and exhausted, trade obstructed and miserably decayed, vast expense and damage to the nation incurred, and many parts of this land spoiled, some of them even to desolation. And for further prosecution of his said evil designs, he, the said Charles Stuart, doth still continue his commissions to the said Prince, and other rebels and revolters, both English and foreigners, and to the Earl of Ormond, and the Irish rebels and revolters associated with him; from whom further invasions upon this land are threatened, upon the procurement, and on the behalf of the said Charles Stuart.

All which wicked designs, wars, and evil practices of him, the said Charles Stuart, have been, and are carried on for the advancement and upholding of a personal interest of will, power, and pretended prerogative to himself and his family, against the public interest, common right, liberty, justice, and peace of the people of this nation, by and from whom he was entrusted as aforesaid.

By all which it appeareth that the said Charles Stuart hath been, and is the occasioner, author, and continuer of the said unnatural, cruel and bloody wars; and therein guilty of all the treasons, murders, rapines, burnings, spoils, desolations, damages and mischiefs to this nation, acted and committed in the said wars, or occasioned thereby.

THE KING'S REASONS FOR REFUSING TO ADMIT THE LEGALITY OF THE COURT

Having already made my protestations, not only against the illegality of this pretended Court, but also, that no earthly power can justly call me (who am your King) in question as a delinquent, I would not any more open my mouth upon this occasion, more than to refer myself to what I have spoken, were I in this case alone concerned: but the duty I owe to God in the preservation of the true liberty of my people will not suffer me at this time to be silent: for, how can any free-born subject of England call life or anything he possesseth his own, if power without right daily make new, and abrogate the old fundamental laws of the land which I now take to be the present case? Wherefore when I came hither, I expected that you would have endeavoured to have satisfied me concerning these grounds which hinder me to answer to your pretended impeachment. But since I see that nothing I can say will move you to it (though negatives are not so naturally proved as affirmatives) yet I will show you the reason why I am confident you cannot judge me, nor indeed the meanest man in England: for I will not (like you) without showing a reason, seek to impose a belief upon my subjects.

There is no proceeding just against any man, but what is warranted, either by God's laws or the municipal laws of the country where he lives. Now I am most confident this day's proceeding cannot be warranted by God's laws; for, on the contrary, the authority of obedience unto Kings is clearly warranted, and strictly commanded in both the Old and New Testament, which, if denied, I am ready instantly to prove.

And for the question now in hand, there it is said, that "where the word of a King is, there is power; and who may say unto him, what dost thou?" Eccles., viii. 4. Then for the law of this land, I am no less confident, that no learned lawyer will affirm that an impeachment can lie against the King, they all going in his name: and one of their maxims is, that the King can do no wrong. Besides, the law upon which you ground your proceedings, must either be old or new: if old, show it; if new, tell what authority, warranted by the fundamental laws of the land, hath made it, and when. But how the House of Commons can erect a Court of Judicature, which was never one itself (as is well known to all lawyers) I leave to God and the world to judge. And it were full as strange, that they should pretend to make laws without King or Lords' House, to any that have heard speak of the laws of England.

And admitting, but not granting, that the people of England's commission could grant your pretended power, I see nothing you can show for that; for certainly you never asked the question of the tenth man in the kingdom, and in this way you manifestly wrong even the poorest ploughman, if you demand not his free consent; nor can you pretend any colour for this your pretended commission, without the consent at least of the major part of every man in England of whatsoever quality or condition, which I am sure you never went about to seek, so far are you from having it. Thus you see that I speak not for my own right alone, as I am your King, but also for the true liberty of all my subjects, which consists, not in the power of government, but in living under such laws, such a government, as may give themselves the best assurance of their lives, and property of their goods; nor in this must or do I forget the privileges of both Houses of Parliament, which this day's proceedings do not only violate, but likewise occasion the greatest breach of their public faith that (I believe) ever was heard of, with which I am far from charging the two Houses; for all the pretended crimes laid against me bear date long before this Treaty at Newport, in which I having concluded as much as in me lay, and hopefully expecting the Houses' agreement thereunto, I was suddenly surprised and hurried from thence as a prisoner; upon which account I am against my will brought hither, where since I am come, I cannot but to my power defend the ancient laws and liberties of this kingdom, together with my own just right. Then for anything I can see, the higher House is totally excluded; and for the House of Commons, it is too well known that the major part of them are detained or deterred from sitting; so as if I had no other, this were sufficient for me to protest against the lawfulness of your pretended Court. Besides all this, the peace of the kingdom is not the least in my thoughts; and what hope of settlement is there, so long as power reigns without rule or law, changing the whole frame of that government under which this kingdom hath flourished for many hundred years? (nor will I say what will fall out in case this lawless, unjust proceeding against me do go on) and believe it, the Commons of England will not thank you for this change; for they will remember how happy they have been of late years under the reigns of Queen Elizabeth, the King my father, and myself, until the beginning of these unhappy troubles, and will have cause to doubt, that they shall never be so happy under any new: and by this time it will be too sensibly evident, that the arms I took up were only to defend the fundamental laws of this kingdom against those who have supposed my power hath totally changed the ancient government.

Thus, having showed you briefly the reasons why I cannot submit to your pretended authority, without violating the trust which I have from God for the welfare and liberty of my people, I expect from you either clear reasons to convince my judgment, showing me that I am in an error (and then truly I will answer) or that you will withdraw your proceedings.

This I intended to speak in Westminster Hall on Monday, January 22, but against reason was hindered to show my reasons.

THE SENTENCE OF THE COURT UPON
THE KING

Whereas the Commons of England assembled in Parliament, have by their late Act intituled an Act of the Commons of England assembled in Parliament, for erecting an High Court of Justice for the trying and judging of Charles Stuart, King of England, authorised and constituted us an High Court of Justice for the trying and judging of the said Charles Stuart for the crimes and treasons in the said Act mentioned; by virtue whereof the said Charles Stuart hath been three several times convented before this High Court, where the first day, being Saturday, the 20th of January instant, in pursuance of the said Act, a charge of high treason and other high crimes was, in the behalf of the people of England, exhibited against him, and read openly unto him, wherein he was charged, that he, the said Charles Stuart, being admitted King of England, and therein trusted with a limited power to govern by, and according to the law of the land, and not otherwise; and by his trust, oath, and office, being obliged to use the power committed to him for the good and benefit of the people, and for the preservation of their rights and liberties; yet, nevertheless, out of a wicked design to erect and uphold in himself an unlimited and tyrannical power to rule according to his will, and to overthrow the rights and liberties of the people, and to take away and make void the foundations thereof, and of all redress and remedy of misgovernment, which by the fundamental constitutions of this kingdom were reserved on the people's behalf in the right and power of frequent and successive Parliaments, or national meetings in Council; he, the said Charles Stuart, for accomplishment of such his designs, and for the protecting of himself and his adherents in his and their wicked practices, to the same end hath traitorously and maliciously levied war against the present Parliament, and people therein represented, as with the circumstances of time and place is in the said charge more particularly set forth; and that he hath thereby caused and procured many thousands of the free people of this nation to be slain; and by divisions, parties, and insurrections within this land, by invasions from foreign parts, endeavoured and procured by him, and by many other evil ways and means, he, the said Charles Stuart, hath not only maintained and carried on the said war both by sea and land, but also hath renewed, or caused to be renewed, the said war against the Parliament and good people of this nation in this present year 1648, in several counties and places in this kingdom in the charge specified; and that he hath for that purpose given his commission to his son the Prince, and others, whereby, besides multitudes of other persons, many such as were by the Parliament entrusted and employed for the safety of this nation, being by him or his agents corrupted to the betraying of their trust, and revolting from the Parliament, have had entertainment and commission for the continuing and renewing of the war and hostility against the said Parliament and people: and that by the said cruel and unnatural war so levied, continued and renewed, much innocent blood of the free people of this nation hath been spilt, many families undone, the public treasure wasted, trade obstructed and miserably decayed, vast expense and damage to the nation incurred, and many parts of the land spoiled, some of them even to desolation; and that he still continues his commission to his said son, and other rebels and revolters, both English and foreigners, and to the Earl of Ormond and to the Irish rebels and revolters associated with him, from whom further invasions of this land are threatened by his procurement and on his behalf; and that all the said wicked designs, wars, and evil practices of him, the said Charles Stuart, were still carried on for the advancement and upholding of the personal interest of will, power, and pretended prerogative to himself and his family, against the public interest, common right, liberty, justice, and peace of the people of this nation; and that he thereby hath been and is the occasioner, author, and continuer of the said unnatural, cruel, and bloody wars, and therein guilty of all the treasons, murders, rapines, burnings, spoils, desolations, damage, and mischief to this nation, acted and committed in the said wars, or occasioned thereby; whereupon the proceedings and judgment of this Court were prayed against him, as a tyrant, traitor, and murderer, and public enemy to the Commonwealth, as by the said charge more fully appeareth. To which charge, being read unto him as aforesaid, he, the said Charles Stuart, was required to give his answer; but he refused so to do, and upon Monday, the 22nd day of January instant, being again brought before this Court, and there required to answer directly to the said charge, he still refused so to do; whereupon his default and contumacy was entered; and the next day, being the third time brought before the Court, judgment was then prayed against him on the behalf of the people of England for his contumacy, and for the matters contained against him in the said charge, as taking the same for confessed, in regard of his refusing to answer thereto; yet notwithstanding this Court (not willing to take advantage of his contempt) did once more require him to answer to the said charge; but he again refused so to do; upon which his several defaults, this Court might justly have proceeded to judgment against him, both for his contumacy and the matters of the charge, taking the same for confessed as aforesaid.

Yet nevertheless this Court, for its own clearer information and further satisfaction, have thought fit to examine witnesses upon oath, and take notice of other evidences, touching the matters contained in the said charge, which accordingly they have done.

Now, therefore, upon serious and mature deliberation of the premises, and consideration had of the notoriety of the matters of fact charged upon him as aforesaid, this Court is in judgment and conscience satisfied that he, the said Charles Stuart, is guilty of levying war against the said Parliament and people, and maintaining and continuing the same; for which in the said charge he stands accused, and by the general course of his government, counsels, and practices, before and since this Parliament began (which have been and are notorious and public, and the effects whereof remain abundantly upon record) this Court is fully satisfied in their judgments and consciences, that he has been and is guilty of the wicked design and endeavours in the said charge set forth; and that the said war hath been levied, maintained, and continued by him as aforesaid, in prosecution, and for accomplishment of the said designs; and that he hath been and is the occasioner, author, and continuer of the said

F

unnatural, cruel, and bloody wars, and therein guilty of high treason, and of the murders, rapines, burnings, spoils, desolations, damage, and mischief to this nation acted and committed in the said war, and occasioned thereby. For all which treasons and crimes this Court doth adjudge that he, the said Charles Stuart, as a tyrant, traitor, murderer, and public enemy to the good people of this nation, shall be put to death by the severing of his head from his body.

(The sentence having been read), His Majesty then said, Will you hear me a word, Sir?

President of the Court   Sir, you are not to be heard after the sentence.

His Majesty   No, Sir?

President   No, Sir, by your favour, Sir. Guards, withdraw your prisoner.

His Majesty   I may speak after sentence, by your favour, Sir, I may speak after sentence, ever. By your favour, hold — the sentence, Sir — I say, Sir, I do — I am not suffered to speak, expect what justice other people may have . . .

JOHN RUSHWORTH, *Historical Collections* (1659–1701)

THE KING'S DEATH WARRANT

At the High Court of Justice for the trying and judging of Charles Stuart, King of England, January 29, Anno Domini 1648.

Whereas Charles Stuart, King of England, is, and standeth convicted, attainted, and condemned of high treason, and other high crimes; and sentence upon Saturday last was pronounced against him by this Court, to be put to death by the severing of his head from his body; of which sentence, execution yet remaineth to be done; these are therefore to will and require you to see the said sentence excuted in the open street before Whitehall, upon the morrow, being the thirtieth day of this instant month of January, between the hours of ten in the morning and five in the afternoon of the same day, with full effect. And for so doing this shall be your sufficient warrant. And these are to require all officers, soldiers, and others, the good people of this nation of England, to be assisting unto you in this service.

To Col. Francis Hacker, Col. Huncks, and Lieut-Col. Phayre, and to every of them.

Given under our hands and seals.

John Bradshaw
Thomas Grey
Oliver Cromwell
and others.

[The King] was sentansed to have his head taken of which the 30 being tusday was dun, on a scaffold at Whitehall near the ban-keating hous, betweene 1 and 2 a clock in the afternoone, when he was on the scaffold a flite of wild ducks came and flew awaye, a drack first staying downe and touching his bill on the block, as many sed that was there by at the time, and sawe the soulders strick and shute at them, but hit none.

Lady Twysden's diary for 1649

ANOTHER CHARACTER OF CHARLES I

. . . yet was not the King satisfied until the whole land was reduced to perfect slavery . . . he thought himself no monarch so long as his will was confined to the bounds of any law; but knowing that the people of England were not pliable to an arbitrary rule, he plotted to subdue them to his yoke by a foreign force, and till he could affect it, made no conscience of granting anything to the people, which he resolved should not oblige him longer than it served his turn: for he was a prince that had nothing of faith or truth, justice or generosity, in him. He was the most obstinate person in his self-will that ever was, and so bent on being an absolute, uncontrollable sovereign that he was resolved either to be such a king or none. His firm adherence to prelacy was not for conscience of one religion more than another, for it was his principle that an honest man might be saved in any profession; but he had a mistaken principle that kingly government in the state could not stand without episcopal government in the church . . .

LUCY HUTCHINSON, *Memoirs of Colonel Hutchinson*
(*c.* 1665; pubd. 1806)

MORE FIGHTING

In the summer of 1648 anti-Parliamentarian revolts broke out in Kent, Essex, and South Wales, part of the Navy mutinied, and the Scots invaded Northern England. The naval mutiny was suppressed, Fairfax put down the revolts in Kent and Essex, Cromwell did the like in Wales, and, most importantly, crushed the Scots in the Battle of Preston as he records in his despatch of the 20th August.

Oliver Cromwell, from Warrington, to the Committee at York, 20th August 1648

We have quite tired out our horses in pursuit of the Enemy; we have killed, taken and disabled all their Foot, and left them only with some Horse, with whom the Duke [of Hamilton] is fled into Delamere Forest, having neither Foot nor Dragooners. They have taken five hundred of them — I mean the Country Forces, as they send me word this day.

They are so tired and in such confusion that if my Horse could but trot after them I could take them all. But we are so weary we can scarce be able to do more than walk after them. I beseech you, therefore, let Sir Henry Cholmley, Sir Edward Rhodes, Colonel Hatcher and Colonel White and all the Countries about you be sent to, to rise with you and follow them. For they are the miserablest party that ever was: I durst engage myself, with Five-hundred fresh Horse and Five-hundred nimble Foot, to destroy them all. My Horse are miserably beaten out; and I have Ten-thousand of them prisoners.

We have killed we know not what, but a very great number, having done execution upon them above thirty miles together — besides what we killed in the two great fights, the one at Preston the other at Warrington. The Enemy was Twenty-four thousand Horse and Foot; whereof Eighteen-thousand Foot and Six-thousand Horse; and our number about Six-thousand Foot and Three-thousand Horse at the utmost.

This is a glorious day: God help England to answer his mercies. I have no more, but beseech you in all your parts to gather into bodies and pursue.

PROCLAMATION

Whereas we are marching with the Parliament's Army into the Kingdom of Scotland, in pursuance of the remaining part of the Enemy who lately invaded the Kingdom of England, and for the recovery of the garrisons of Berwick and Carlisle:

These are to declare, That if any officer or soldier under my command shall take or demand any money, or shall violently take any horses, goods, or victuals without order, or shall abuse the people in any sort, he shall be tried by a Council of War; and the said person so offending shall be punished according to the Articles of War made for the government of the Army in the Kingdom of England, which punishment is death.

Each Colonel or other Chief Officer in every Regiment is to transcribe a copy of this, and to cause the same to be delivered to each Captain in his Regiment; and every said Captain of each respective troop and company is to publish the same to his troop or company, and to take a strict course that nothing be done contrary hereunto.

Given under my hand, this 20th September 1648.

Oliver Cromwell

The angry mood of the Second Civil War is illustrated by the harsher treatment of prisoners.

Edmund Verney to Sir Ralph Verney, 14th September 1648

... The Parliament are selling the Scots common prisoners to the Barbadoes and other plantations, which I conceive to be about 12,000 or 14,000 men, and article the merchants for their not returning. I think they mean to transplant the whole nation of the Scots ...

Dr. Kirkton, writing from Paris

The Scots are sold at London to those who have plantations for 5l. the score.

In the summer of 1649 Cromwell was asked to take command in Ireland, where the situation was desperate. He acted effectively, subjugating the country, but with a barbarity that is still remembered in Ireland.

Oliver Cromwell, from Dublin, to the Speaker of the Parliament of England, 17th September 1649

... Divers of the Enemy retreated into the Mill Mount, a place very strong and of difficult access, being exceedingly high, having a good graft, and strongly palisadoed. The Governor, Sir Arthur Ashton, and divers considerable officers being there, our men getting up to them were ordered by me to put them all to the sword. And indeed, being in the heat of action, I forbade them to spare any that were in arms in the town; and I think that night they put to the sword about 2000 men; divers of the officers and soldiers being fled over the bridge into the other part of the town, where about 100 of them possessed St. Peter's church steeple, some the West Gate, and others a strong round tower next the gate called St. Sunday's. These, being summoned to yield to mercy, refused.

Whereupon I ordered the steeple of St. Peter's Church to be fired, when one of them was heard to say in the midst of the flames, "God damn me, God confound me, I burn, I burn."

The next day the other two towers were summoned . . . When [at length] they submitted, their officers were knocked on the head; and every tenth man of the soldiers killed, and the rest shipped for the Barbadoes. The soldiers in the other tower were all spared as to their lives only, and shipped likewise for the Barbadoes.

I am persuaded that this is a righteous judgment of God upon these barbarous wretches, who have imbrued their hands in so much innocent blood, and that it will tend to prevent the effusion of blood for the future. Which are the satisfactory grounds to such actions, which otherwise cannot but work remorse and regret . . .

And now give me leave to say how this work is wrought. It was set upon some of our hearts, That a great thing should be done, not by power or might, but by the Spirit of God. And is it not so, clearly? That which caused your men to storm so courageously, it was the Spirit of God, who gave your men courage, and took it away again; and gave the Enemy courage and took it away again; and gave your men courage again, and therewith this happy success. And therefore it is good that God alone have all the glory.

It is remarkable that these people, at the first, set up the Mass in some places of the town that had been monasteries: but afterwards grew so insolent that, the last Lord's Day before the storm, the Protestants were thrust out of the great church called St. Peter's, and they had public Mass there: and in this very place near 1000 of them were put to the sword, fleeing thither for safety. I believe all their friars were knocked on the head promiscuously but two, the one of which was Father Peter Taaff, brother to the Lord Taaff, whom the soldiers took the next day and made an end of. The other was taken in the round tower, under the repute of a Lieutenant, and when he understood that the officers in that tower had no quarter, he confessed he was a friar; but that did not save him.

Oliver Cromwell to the Governor of Ross, 19th October 1649

... For that which you mention concerning liberty of conscience, I meddle not with any man's conscience. But if by liberty of conscience you mean a liberty to exercise the Mass, I judge it best to use plain dealing and let you know, where the Parliament of England have power that will not be allowed of ...

Six days after the execution of Charles I, the Estates in Scotland proclaimed Charles, Prince of Wales, King of Great Britain, France, and Ireland. Charles II was in exile in the Netherlands at the time, and it was not until 1650 that the hard bargaining between him and the Scots came to an end and he was allowed to return to his Scottish kingdom. The terms which he was forced to accept were humiliating: acceptance of the Solemn League and Covenant, a promise to impose Presbyterianism throughout Great Britain and Ireland, and a public denunciation of the actions of his father and his mother. Cromwell led an English army into Scotland and, on the 3rd September 1650, defeated the Scottish army at Dunbar. In the summer of 1651 Charles marched southwards and crossed the border into England, but the hoped-for support from the English did not materialise. The Royalist and Parliamentarian armies came to grips at Worcester, exactly one year after the Battle of Dunbar.

Oliver Cromwell, from near Worcester, to the Speaker of the Parliament of England. 3rd September 1651 (10 at night)

Being so weary and scarce able to write, yet I thought it my duty to let you know thus much. That upon this day, being the 3rd September (remarkable for a mercy vouchsafed to your forces on this day twelvemonth in Scotland) we built a bridge over Severn, between it and Teme, about half a mile from Worcester: and

another over Teme within pistol-shot of our other bridge. Lieutenant-General Fleetwood and Major-General Dean marched from
Upton on the south-west side of Severn up to Powick, a town which
was a pass the enemy kept. We passed over some horse and foot,
and were in conjunction with the Lieutenant-General's forces. We
beat the enemy from hedge to hedge until we beat him into Worcester.

The enemy then drew all his forces on the other side of the town,
all but what he had lost, and made a very considerable fight with us
for three hours space: but in the end we beat him totally, and
pursued him to his royal fort, which we took; and indeed have
beaten his whole army. When we took this fort we turned his own
guns upon him. The enemy hath had great loss: and certainly is
scattered and run several ways. We are in pursuit of him, and have
laid forces in several places that we hope will gather him up.

Indeed this hath been a very glorious mercy, and as stiff a contest
for four or five hours as ever I have seen. Both your old forces and
those new-raised have behaved themselves with very great courage;
and He that made them come out made them willing to fight for
you. The Lord God Almighty frame our hearts to real thankfulness for this, which is alone His doing. I hope I shall within a day or
two give you a more perfect account.

*The romantic story of Charles's escape after the Battle of Worcester is
well known. Here is his own account, as retold nine years later and
recorded by Pepys.*

23rd May 1660. All the afternoon the King walked here and there,
up and down, very active and stirring. Upon the quarter-deck he
fell into discourse of his escape from Worcester, where it made me
ready to weep to hear the stories that he told of his difficulties that
he passed through; as his travelling four days and three nights on
foot, every step up to his knees in dirt, with nothing but a green
coat and a pair of country breeches on, and a pair of country shoes

that made him so sore all over his feet that he could scarce stir; yet he was forced to run away from a miller and other company, that took them for rogues. His sitting at table at one place, where the master of the house, that had not seen him in eight years, did know him, but kept it private; when at the same table there was one that had been of his own regiment at Worcester could not know him, but made him drink the King's health, and said that the King was at least four fingers higher than he. At another place he was by some servants of the house made to drink, that they might know him not to be a Roundhead, which they swore he was. In another place, at his inn, the master of the house, as the King was standing with his hands on the back of a chair by the fire-side, kneeled down and kissed his hand privately, saying that he would not ask him who he was, but bid God bless him whither he was going. Then the difficulty of getting a boat to get into France, where he was fain to plot with the master thereof to keep his design from the four men and a boy (which was all his ship's company) and so got to Fécamp in France.

Pepys' Diary

THE INTERREGNUM

It was easier to remove the monarch than to find a new and acceptable form of government. The next eleven years saw a series of constitutional experiments, from the rule of the Rump, to the rule of Cromwell and a nominated Parliament, to the First Protectorate of Cromwell with an elected Parliament, to the Major-Generals ruling the eleven military districts of England under the Protector, to Cromwell's refusal of Parliament's offer of the title of King but his acceptance of the Humble Petition and Advice, and the inauguration of the Second Protectorate in 1657. After Cromwell's death on 3rd September 1658, his son, Richard, was made Protector. He was more in need of protection himself than able to extend it to others, and he willingly resigned in May 1659. The months of constitutional confusion which ensued were brought to an end when General Monk decided in favour of recalling the full Parliament, knowing that it would bring about the Stuart restoration.

ACT DECLARING ENGLAND TO BE A COMMONWEALTH, 19th MAY 1649

Be it declared and enacted by this present Parliament, and by the authority of the same, that the people of England, and of all the dominions and territories thereunto belonging, are and shall be, and are hereby constituted, made, established, and confirmed, to be a Commonwealth and Free State, and shall from henceforth be governed as a Commonwealth and Free State by the supreme authority of this nation, the representatives of the people in Parliament, and by such as they shall appoint and constitute as officers and ministers under them for the good of the people, and that without any King or House of Lords.

An account of the divisions and differences in the country.

J.R., from England, to Sir Ralph Verney, in exile in France,
14th February 1650

I am much ashamed to be so long in performing my promise to
write you an account of affairs here. (1st) As to the Presbyterian
party, they were never more aggrieved . . . Take the new Engagement they cannot, because it is (they say) expressly contrary to the
Covenant, and if they do not they must starve and beg . . . I (who
have taken this Engagement) . . . willingly would have no more
Oaths nor Engagements by compulsion, till we have either kept
what we have taken or repented for what we have broken. (2)
As to the Independent party, many of which are truly Godly and
pious, their number increases little, because Atheism increases so
fast; for indeed many who had great knowledge in spiritual things
are now puffed up with vain fancies to live above ordinances, yea
above the Scriptures, and at last declare vice to be virtue, that God
sees no sin; a sad generation of people. This puts me in mind of the
(3rd) sort of people, I mean the Levellers, most of which party have
been cordial against the common enemy, yet of principles inconsistent with the word of God . . . for, but four days since, the
Council of State sent to apprehend a grand Leveller, who upon the
approach of the first messenger stabbed him to the heart with a
dagger, and so he did the second, laid him dead on the ground also;
and the third he mortally wounded, who is also since dead . . .
My (4th and) last party I shall instance are the Cavaliers, whose
wisdom and necessity, rather than goodwill, inclines them to be
quiet. The better sort will hardly stir, the lower sort of squires . . .
are ready to rise, so great are their wants; an Act of Oblivion with a
condition of good behaviour (else to forfeit it) would do good,
but 'tis petty treason to speak it . . .

Parliament tried to persuade Cromwell to accept the title of King, and for some time he gave no definite answer; finally —

Speech of Oliver Cromwell, Lord Protector, to the Parliament, at the Banqueting House, Whitehall, 8th May 1657

. . . I should not be an honest man if I did not tell you that I cannot accept of the Government, nor undertake the trouble and charge of it . . . with the title of King. And that is mine answer to this great and weighty business.

THE HUMBLE PETITION AND ADVICE
25th MAY 1657

To his Highness the Lord Protector of the Commonwealth of England, Scotland and Ireland, and the dominions thereto belonging; the Humble Petition and Advice of the Knights, Citizens and Burgesses now assembled in the Parliament of this Commonwealth.

We, the knights, citizens and burgesses in this present Parliament assembled, taking into our most serious consideration the present state of these three nations, joined and united under your Highness' protection, cannot but in the first place, with all thankfulness, acknowledge the wonderful mercy of Almighty God in delivering us from that tyranny and bondage, both in our spiritual and civil concernments, which the late King and his party designed to bring us under . . . we have judged it a duty incumbent upon us, to present and declare these our most just and necessary desires to your Highness.

1.   That your Highness will be pleased by and under the name and style of Lord Protector of the Commonwealth of England, Scotland and Ireland, and the dominions and territories thereunto belonging, to hold and exercise the office of Chief Magistrate of these nations, and to govern according to this petition and advice in all things therein contained, and in all other things according to the

laws of these nations, and not otherwise; that your Highness will be pleased during your lifetime to appoint and declare the person who shall, immediately after your death, succeed you in the Government of these nations.

.   .   .   .

BEGINNING OF THE SECOND PROTECTORATE

27th June 1657. Yesterday His Highness was in Westminster Hall with the Parliament, the Lord Mayor and Aldermen and the Judges, where he took an oath and was proclaimed Lord Protector of England, Scotland and Ireland, with three great shouts made by the soldiers and some few others. I was there and saw him in his King-like robes. He came through the Hall in great state.

Roger Fleming's note-book

Speech of Oliver Cromwell, Lord Protector, to the Parliament, 4th February 1658

. . . It hath been not only your endeavour to pervert the Army while you have been sitting and to draw them to state the question about a Commonwealth, but some of you have been listing of persons, by commission of Charles Stuart, to join with any insurrection that may be made. And what is like to come upon this, the Enemy being ready to invade us, but even present blood and confusion? And if this be so, I do assign [it] to this cause: Your not assenting to what you did invite me to by your Petition and Advice, as that which might prove the Settlement of the Nation. And if this be the end of your sitting, and this be your carriage, I think it high time that an end be put to your sitting. And I do dissolve this Parliament. And let God be judge between you and me.

Cromwell died of a tertian ague on the 3rd September 1658, the anniversary of his victories at Dunbar and Worcester.

THE LYING-IN-STATE OF CROMWELL

One of the first acts of the new Government was to order the funeral of the late usurper; and the Council having resolved that it should be very magnificent, the care of it was referred to a Committee of them, who, sending for Mr Kinnersly, master of the Wardrobe, desired him to find out some precedent by which they might govern themselves in this important affair. After examination of his books and papers Mr Kinnersly, who was suspected to be inclined to Popery, recommended to them the solemnities used upon the like occasion for Philip the Second, King of Spain, who had been represented to be in Purgatory for about two months. In the like manner was the body of this great Reformer laid in Somerset House: the apartment was hung with black, the daylight was excluded, and no other but that of wax tapers to be seen. This scene of Purgatory continued till the first of November, which being the day preceding that commonly called All Souls, he was removed into the great Hall of the said House, and represented in effigy, standing on a bed of crimson velvet covered with a gown of the like coloured velvet, a sceptre in his hand, and a crown on his head. That part of the Hall wherein the Bed stood was railed in, and the rails and ground within them covered with crimson velvet. Four or five hundred candles set in flat shining candlesticks were so placed round near the roof of the hall that the light they gave seemed like the rays of the sun: by all which he was represented to be now in a state of glory. This folly and profusion so far provoked the People that they threw dirt in the night on his Escutcheon, that was placed over the great gate of Somerset House. I purposely omit the rest of the Pageantry, the great number of persons that attended on the body, the procession to Westminster, the vast expense in Mourning, the state and magnificence of the Monument erected for him, with many other things that I care not to remember.

EDMUND LUDLOW (1617–92), *Memoirs* (1698)

THREE ASSESSMENTS OF THE CHARACTER
OF CROMWELL

Never man was highlier extolled, and never man was baselier reported of, and vilified than this man. No (mere) man was *better* and *worse* spoken of than he; according as men's interests led their judgments. The soldiers and sectaries most highly magnified him, till he began to seek the Crown and the establishment of his family; and then, there were so many that would be half-kings themselves, that a king did seem intolerable to them. The Royalists abhorred him as a most perfidious hypocrite; and the Presbyterians [as was Baxter himself] thought him little better, in his management of public matters.

. . . I think that . . . he meant honestly in the main, and was pious and conscionable in the main course of his life, till prosperity and success corrupted him; that, at his first entrance into the Wars, being but a captain of horse, he had a special care to get religious men into his troop . . . it was the very esteem and love of religious men that principally moved him, and the avoiding those disorders, mutinies, plunderings and grievances of the country which debauched men in armies are commonly guilty of. By this means he indeed sped better than he expected . . . Both piety and ambition concurred in his countenancing of all that he thought Godly, of what sect soever; piety pleadeth for them as Godly, and Charity as men; and ambition secretly telleth him what use he might make of them. He meaneth well in all this at the beginning, and thinketh he doth all for the safety of the Godly, and the public good, but not without an eye to himself.

When success had broken down all considerable opposition, he was then in the face of his strongest temptations, which conquered him when he had conquered others. He thought that he had hitherto done well, both as to the end and means, and God by the wonderful blessing of his Providence had owned his endeavours, and it was none but God that had made him great . . . He thought it lawful to use his wits, to choose each instrument, and suit each means unto its end; and accordingly he daily employed himself, and modelled the Army, and disbanded all other garrisons and forces and committees which were like to have hindered his design . . .

Having thus forced his conscience to justify all his cause (the cutting off the King, the setting up himself and his adherents, the pulling down the Parliament and the Scots), he thinketh that the end being good and necessary, the necessary means cannot be bad . . .

He seemed exceeding open-hearted, by a familiar rustic affected carriage (especially to his soldiers in sporting with them); but he thought secrecy a virtue and dissimulation no vice, and simulation — that is, in plain English, a lie — or perfidiousness to be a tolerable fault in a case of necessity; being of the same opinion with the Lord Bacon (who was not so precise as learned) that *the best composition and temperature is to have openness in fame and opinion, secrecy in habit, dissimulation in seasonable use; and a power to feign if there be no remedy.* Therefore he kept fair with all, saving his open or unreconcileable enemies. He carried it with such dissimulation that Anabaptists, Independents, and Antinomians did all think that he was one of them; but he never endeavoured to persuade the Presbyterians that he was one of them, but only that he would do them justice, and preserve them, and that he honoured their worth and piety; for he knew that they were not so easily deceived.

RICHARD BAXTER (1615–91), *Reliquiae Baxterianae* (1696)

Cromwell (though the greatest dissembler living) always made his hypocrisy of singular use and benefit to him, and never did anything, how ungracious or imprudent soever it seemed to be, but what was necessary to the design; even his roughness and unpolishedness which in the beginning of the Parliament he affected . . . was necessary, and his first public declaration in the beginning of the War, to his troop when it was first mustered — that he would not deceive or cozen them by the perplexed and involved expressions in his Commission to fight for King and Parliament, and therefore told them that, if the King chanced to be in the body of the enemy that he was to charge, he would as soon discharge his pistol upon him as at any other private person, and if their conscience would not permit them to do the like, he advised them not to list themselves in his troop or under his command — which was generally looked upon as imprudent and malicious, and might by the professions the Parliament then made have proved dangerous to him, yet served his turn, and severed and united all the furious and incensed men against the government, whether ecclesiastical or civil, to look upon him as a man for their turn, and upon whom they might depend as one who would go through his work that he undertook; and his strict and unsociable humour in not keeping company with the other officers of the Army in their jollities and excesses . . drew all those of the like sour or reserved natures to his society and conversation . . . He grew to have a wonderful interest in the common soldiers, out of which, as his authority increased, he made all his officers, well instructed how to live in the same manner with their soldiers that they might be able to apply them to their own purposes . . .

He could never have done half that mischief without great parts of courage and industry and judgment . . . Without doubt no man with more wickedness ever attempted anything, or brought to pass what he desired more wickedly, more in the face and contempt of religion and moral honesty, yet wickedness as great as his could never have accomplished those trophies without the assistance of a great spirit, an admirable circumspection and sagacity, and a most magnanimous resolution . . .

// He was not a man of blood, and totally declined Machiavelli's method, which prescribes on any alteration of a government, as a thing absolutely necessary, to cut of all the heads of those and extirpate their families who are friends to the old, and it was confidently reported that in the Council of Officers it was more than once proposed that there might be a general massacre of all the royal party as the only expedient to secure the government, but Cromwell would never consent to it, it may be out of too much contempt of his enemies. In a word, as he had all the wickednesses against which damnation is denounced and for which Hell-fire is prepared, so he had some virtues which have caused the memory of some men in all ages to be celebrated, and he will be looked upon by posterity as a brave, bad man.

CLARENDON, *History of the Rebellion* (1646–71; pubd. 1702–4)

John Maidston [Cromwell's former servant] from Westminster, to John Winthrop, Governor of Connecticut, 24th March 1659

His body was well compact and strong, his stature under 6 feet (I believe about two inches), his head so shaped as you might see it a storehouse and shop of a vast treasury of natural parts. His temper exceeding fiery, as I have known, but the flame of it kept down for the most part, or soon allayed with those moral endowments he had. He was naturally compassionate towards objects in distress, even to an effeminate measure; though God had made him a heart wherein was left little room of any fear but what was due to Himself, of which there was a large proportion, yet did he exceed in tenderness towards sufferers. A larger soul, I think, hath seldom dwelt in a house of clay than his was. I do believe, if this story were impartially transmitted and the unprejudiced world well possessed with it, she would add him to her nine worthies and make up that number a decemviri. He lived and died in comfortable communion with God, as judicious persons near him well observed. He was that Mordecai that sought the welfare of his people, and spake peace to his seed, yet were his temptations such, as it appeared frequently, that he, that hath grace enough for many men, may have too little for himself; the treasure he had being but in an earthen vessel, and that equally defiled with original sin, as any other man's nature is.

THE STUARTS RESTORED

11th February 1660. At noon I walked in [Westminster] Hall, where I heard the news of a letter from Monk, who did resolve to stand for the sudden filling up of the House, and it was very strange how the countenance of men in the Hall was all changed with joy in half an hour's time . . .

Pepys' Diary

Upon the opening of the Parliament, viz. letting in the secluded members, he [William Prynne] girt on his old long rusty sword (longer than ordinary). Sir William Waller marching behind him (as he went to the House) W. Prynne's long sword ran between Sir William's short legs, and threw him down, which caused laughter.

JOHN AUBREY (1626–97), *Brief Lives*

5th March 1660 . . . Great hopes of the King's coming again.
6th March 1660 . . . Every body now drinks the King's health without any fear, whereas before it was very private that a man dare do it.
16th March 1660 . . . now they begin to talk loud of the King . . .

Pepys' Diary

THE DECLARATION OF BREDA

Charles, by the grace of God, King of England, Scotland, France and Ireland, Defender of the Faith, &c. To all our loving subjects, of what degree or quality soever, greeting.

.   .   .   .

And to the end that the fear of punishment may not engage any, conscious to themselves of what is past, to a perseverance in guilt for the future, by opposing the quiet and happiness of their country, in the restoration of King, Peers and people to their just, ancient and fundamental rights, we do, by these presents, declare, that we do grant a free and general pardon, which we are ready, upon demand, to pass under our Great Seal of England, to all our subjects, of what degree or quality soever, who, within forty days after the publishing hereof, shall lay hold upon this our grace and favour, and shall, by any public act, declare their doing so, and that they return to the loyalty and obedience of good subjects; excepting only such persons as shall hereafter be excepted by Parliament, those only to be excepted   .   .   .   .

And because the passion and uncharitableness of the times have produced several opinions in religion, by which men are engaged in parties and animosities against each other (which, when they shall hereafter unite in a freedom of conversation, will be composed or better understood), we do declare a liberty to tender consciences, and that no man shall be disquieted or called in question for differences of opinion in matter of religion, which do not disturb the peace of the kingdom;   .   .   .   .

And because, in the continued distractions of so many years, and so many and great revolutions, many grants and purchases of estates have been made to and by many officers, soldiers and others, who are now possessed of the same, and who may be liable to actions at law upon several titles, we are likewise willing that all such differences, and all things relating to such grants, sales and purchases, shall be determined in Parliament, which can best provide for the just satisfaction of all men who are concerned.

. . . .

Given under our Sign Manual and Privy Signet, at our Court at Breda, this 4/14 day of April, 1660, in the twelfth year of our reign.

2nd May 1660 . . . Great joy all yesterday at London, and at night more bonfires than ever, and ringing of bells, and drinking of the King's health upon their knees in the streets, which methinks is a little too much. But everybody seems to be very joyful in the business, insomuch that our sea-commanders now begin to say so too, which a week ago they would not do. And our seamen, as many as had money or credit for drink, did do nothing else this evening.

16th May 1660 . . . And how overjoyed the King was when Sir J. Greenville brought him some money [to the Netherlands]; so joyful that he called the Princess Royal and Duke of York to look upon it as it lay in the portmanteau before it was taken out.

Pepys' Diary

Being come aboard one of the fairest of those ships which attended at Sluys for wafting him over from the Hague in Holland; and therein having taken leave of his sisters, the Princess Royal; he set sail for England on Wednesday evening, May 23rd, 1660. And having, during his abode at sea, given new names to that whole navy (consisting of twenty-six goodly vessels), he arrived at Dover on the Friday following [May 25th] about two o'clock in the afternoon.

Ready on the shore to receive him, stood the Lord General Monk, as also the Earl of Winchelsea, Constable of Dover Castle,

with divers persons of quality on the one hand; and the Mayor of
Dover, accompanied by his brethren of that Corporation of the
other, with a rich canopy. As soon as he had set foot on the shore,
the Lord General presenting himself before him on his knee, and
kissing his royal hand; was embraced by his Majesty: and received
divers gracious expressions of the great sense he had of his loyalty,
and in being so instrumental in his Restoration.

There also did the Corporation of Dover, and the Earl of
Winchelsea do their duties to him, in like sort; all the people
making joyful shouts: the great guns from the ships and castle
telling aloud the happy news of this his entrance upon English
ground.

From thence, taking coach immediately, with his royal brothers,
the Dukes of York and Gloucester, he passed to Barham Down — a
great plain lying betwixt Dover and Canterbury — where were
drawn up divers gallant troops of horse, consisting of the nobility,
knights and gentlemen of note, clad in very rich apparel; commanded by the Duke of Buckingham, Earls of Oxford, Derby,
Northampton, Winchelsea, Lichfield, and the Lord Viscount
Mordaunt: As also the several foot regiments of the Kentish men.
Being entered the Down on horseback, where multitudes of the
country people stood making loud shouts, he rode to the head of
each troop — they being placed on his left hand, three deep — who
bowing to him, kissed the hilts of their swords, and then flourished
them above their heads, with no less acclamations; the trumpets
in the meantime also echoing the like to them.

In the suburb of Canterbury stood the Mayor and Aldermen of
that ancient city, who received him with loud music, and presented
him with a cup of gold of two hundred and fifty pounds value.
Whence, after a speech made to him by the Recorder, he passed to
the Lord Campden's house, the Mayor carrying the sword before
him.

. . . .

From Canterbury he came on Monday to Rochester, where the
people had hung up, over the midst of the streets, as he rode, many

beautiful garlands, curiously made up with costly scarves and ribbons, decked with spoons and bodkins of silver, and small plate of several sorts; and some with gold chains, in like sort as at Canterbury: each striving to outdo the other in all expressions of joy.

On Tuesday, May the 29th (which happily fell out to be the anniversary of his Majesty's birthday) he set forth from Rochester in his coach; but afterwards took horse on the farther side of Blackheath: on which spacious plain he found divers great and eminent troops of horse, in a most splendid and glorious equipage; and a kind of rural triumph, expressed by the country swains, in a morris dance with the old music of taber and pipe; which was performed with all agility and cheerfulness imaginable.

And from this Heath these troops marched off before him; viz. Major General Brown, the Merchant Adventurers, Alderman Robinson, the Lord Maynard, the Earls of Norwich, Peterborough, Cleveland, Derby, Duke of Richmond, and His Majesty's own Life Guards.

In this order proceeding towards London, there were placed in Deptford, on his right hand — as he passed through the town — above an hundred proper maids, clad all alike in white garments, with scarves above them: who having prepared many flaskets covered with fine linen, and adorned with rich scarves and ribbons; which flaskets were full of flowers and sweet herbs, strewed the way before him as he rode.

From thence passing on he came into Saint George's Fields in Southwark, where the Lord Mayor and Aldermen of London in their scarlet, with the Recorder and other City Council, waited for him in a large tent, hung with tapestry; in which they had placed a chair of state, with a rich canopy over it. When he came thither the Lord Mayor presented him with the City sword, and the Recorder made a speech to him; which being done, he alighted and went into the tent, where a noble banquet was prepared for him.

. . . .

In this magnificent fashion, His Majesty entered the Borough of Southwark, about half-past three o'clock in the afternoon; and within an hour after, the City of London, at the Bridge: where he found the windows and streets exceedingly thronged with people to behold him, and the wall adorned with hangings and carpets of tapestry and other costly stuff: and in many places sets of loud music; all the conduits as he passed running claret wine; and the several Companies in their liveries, with the ensigns belonging to them; as also the trained bands of the city standing along the streets as he passed, welcoming him with loyal acclamations.

And within the rails where Charing Cross formerly was, a stand of six hundred pikes, consisting of knights and gentlemen, as had been officers in the armies of his late Majesty, of blessed memory: the truly noble and valiant Sir John Stowell, Knight of the Honourable Order of the Bath (a person famous for his eminent actings and sufferings) being in the head of them.

From which place, the citizens in velvet coats and gold chains being drawn up on each hand, and divers companies of foot soldiers; his Majesty passed betwixt them, and entered White Hall at seven o'clock: the people making loud shouts, and the horse and foot several volleys of shots, at this his happy arrival. Where the House of Lords and Commons of Parliament received him, and kissed his royal hand.

At the same time likewise, the Reverend Bishops of Ely, Salisbury, Rochester and Chichester in their episcopal habits, with divers of the long oppressed orthodox clergy; met in that royal Chapel of King Henry the Seventh of Westminster, and there also sung Te DEUM &c., in praise and thanks to Almighty GOD, for this His unspeakable mercy, in the deliverance of his Majesty from many dangers, and so happily restoring him to rule these kingdoms according to his just and undoubted right.

England's Joy, or a Relation of the Most Remarkable passages, from His Majesty's Arrival at Dover, to His entrance at Whitehall.

29th May 1660 . . . I stood in the Strand and beheld it and blessed God. And all this was done without one drop of blood shed, and by that very army which rebelled against him; but it was the Lord's doing, for such a Restoration was never mentioned in any history, ancient or modern, since the return of the Jews from the Babylonish captivity; nor so joyful a day and so bright ever seen in this nation, this happening when to expect or to effect it was past all human policy.

Evelyn's Diary

KING CHARLES II's PROGRESS: COMPULSORY ATTENDANCE ORDER

Whereas the King's Majesty is now upon his progress in coming into this country, it is therefore ordered and decreed at this present Assembly that a treatment shall be made and presented to him . . . and that the Mayor, Jurats, and Common Council of this town shall be then and there attending in their formalities, upon pain of 20s. for every Jurat making default then and there and 10s. for every commoner making default then and there excepting only such Jurats and commoners as shall be excused by Mr. Mayor.

Order made by Faversham Corporation, 26th October 1660

2nd November 1660 . . . I observed this night very few bonfires in the City, not above three in all London, for the Queen's coming; whereby I guess that (as I believed before) her coming do please but very few.

Pepys' Diary

AFTERMATH OF THE RESTORATION

1660 October 13. I went out to Charing Cross to see Major General Harrison hanged, drawn, and quartered, which was done there, he looking as cheerful as any man could do in that condition. He was presently cut down, and his head and his heart shown to the people, at which there was great shouts of joy. Thus it was my chance to see the King beheaded at Whitehall and to see the first blood shed in revenge for the King at Charing Cross.

October 20. This afternoon I saw limbs of some of our new traitors set upon Aldersgate, which was a sad sight to see; and a bloody week this and the last have been, there being ten hanged, drawn and quartered.

December 4. This day the Parliament voted that the bodies of Oliver, Ireton, Bradshaw, etc., should be taken up out of their graves in the Abbey, and drawn to the gallows, and there hanged and buried under it; which (methinks) do trouble me, that a man of so great courage as he was should have that dishonour, though otherwise he might deserve it enough.

Pepys' Diary

THE CHARACTER OF CHARLES II

One great objection made to him was the concealing himself and disguising his thoughts. In this there ought a latitude to be given; it is a defect not to have it at all, and a fault to have it too much. Human nature will not allow the mean; like all other things, as soon as ever men get to do them well, they cannot easily hold from doing them too much. 'Tis the case even in the least things, as singing, etc. . . . The vulgar definition of dissembling is downright lying; that kind of it which is less ill-bred cometh pretty near to it. Only Princes and persons of honour must have gentler words given to their faults than the nature of them may in themselves deserve. Princes dissemble with too many not to have it discovered; no wonder, then, that he carried it so far that it was discovered. Men compared notes . . . Those who knew his face fixed their eyes there, and thought it of more importance to see, than to hear what he said. His face was as little a blab as most men's, yet though it could not be called a prattling face, it would sometimes tell tales to a good observer.

His wit consisted chiefly in the quickness of his apprehension. His apprehension made him find faults, and that led him to short sayings upon them, not always equal but often very good.

By his being abroad he contracted a habit of conversing familiarly, which, added to his natural genius, made him very apt to talk, perhaps more than a very nice judgment would approve.

He was apter to make *broad allusions* upon any thing that gave the least occasion than was altogether suitable with the very good breeding he showed in most other things. The company he kept whilst abroad had so used him to that sort of dialect that he was so far from thinking it a fault or an indecency that he made it a matter of raillery upon those who could not prevail upon themselves to join in it.

. . . The hypocrisy of the former times inclined men to think they could not show too great an aversion to it, and that helped to encourage this unbounded liberty of talking, without the restraints of decency which were before observed. In his more familiar conversations with the ladies, even they must be passive, if they would not enter into it. . . . The thing called wit a Prince may taste, but it is dangerous for him to take too much of it . . . there is a charm in wit which a Prince must resist, and that to him was no easy matter; it was contesting with Nature upon terms of disadvantage.

He encouraged some to talk a good deal more with him than one would have expected from a man of so good a taste; he should rather have ordered his Attorney-General to have prosecuted them for a misdemeanour, in using common-sense so scurvily in his presence . . .

It fell out rather by accident than choice that his mistresses were such as did not care that wit of the best kind should have the precedence in their apartments . . .

His affability was a part, and perhaps not the least, of his wit . . . There was at first as much of art as nature in his affability, but by habit it became natural. It is an error of the better hand, but the *universality* taketh away a good deal of the force of it . . . at last it cometh to smile for smile, meaning nothing of either side, without any kind of effect, mere drawing-room compliments . . .

His wit was better suited to his condition before he was restored than afterwards. The wit of a gentleman and that of a crowned Head ought to be two different things. As there is a crown law there is a crown wit too. To use it with reserve is very good, and very rare. There is a dignity in doing things seldom, even without any other circumstance. Where wit run continually the spring is apt to fail, so that it groweth vulgar and the more it is practised the more it is debased.

He was so good at finding out men's weak sides that it made him less intent to cure his own; that generally happeneth . . .

He had a *mechanical* head, which appeared in his inclination to shipping and fortification, etc. He had a very good memory, though he would not always make equal good use of it . . . His chain of memory was longer than his chain of thought; the first could bear any burden, the other was tired by being carried on too long; it was fit to ride a heat but it had not wind enough for a long course.

A very great memory often forgetteth how much time is lost by repeating things of no use. It was one reason of his talking so much; since a great memory will always have something to say, and will be discharging itself, whether in or out of season, if a good judgment doth not go along with it to make it stop or turn . . . Sometimes he would make shrewd applications, etc., at others he would bring things out of [his memory] that never deserved to be laid in it . . .

It was not the best use he made of his backstairs to admit men to bribe him against himself, to procure a defalcation, help a lame accountant to get off, or side with the farmers [*i.e.* tax-gatherers] against the improvement of the Revenue. The King was made the instrument to defraud the Crown, which is somewhat extraordinary . . .

He could not properly be said to be either covetous or liberal; his desire to get was not with an intention to be rich, and his spending was rather an easiness in letting money go than any premeditated thought for the distribution of it. He would do as much to throw off the burden of a present importunity as he would to relieve a want . . . He had as little eagerness to oblige as he had to hurt men . . . This principle of making the love of ease exercise an entire sovereignty in his thoughts would have been less censured in a private man than might be in a Prince . . .

It must be allowed he had a little over-balance on the well-natured side, not vigour enough to be earnest to do a kind thing much less to do a harsh one; but if a hard thing was done to another man, he did not eat his supper the worse for it . . .

In short, this Prince might more properly be said to have *gifts* than *virtues*, as affability, easiness of living, inclinations to give and forgive: qualities that flowed from his nature rather than from his virtue.

He had not more application to any thing than the preservation of his health; it had an entire preference to anything else in his thoughts, and he might be said without aggravation to study that with as little intermission as any man in the world. He understood it very well, only in this he failed, that he thought it was more reconcileable with his pleasure than it really was.

HALIFAX (1633–95), *A Character of King Charles the Second*
(pubd. 1750)